AAT

Credit Management
Level 4
Course Book
For assessments from
1 September 2016

First edition June 2016

ISBN 9781 4727 4826 3
ISBN (for internal use only) 9781 4727 4882 9

British Library Cataloguing-in-Publication Data
A catalogue record for this book is available from the
British Library

Published by

BPP Learning Media Ltd
BPP House, Aldine Place
142-144 Uxbridge Road
London W12 8AA

www.bpp.com/learningmedia

Printed in the United Kingdom by RICOH UK Limited
Unit 2
Wells Place
Merstham
RH1 3LG

> Your learning materials, published by BPP Learning Media
> Ltd, are printed on paper obtained from traceable
> sustainable sources.

BPP Learning Media is grateful to the IASB for permission to
reproduce extracts from the International Financial Reporting
Standards including all International Accounting Standards,
SIC and IFRIC Interpretations (the Standards). The Standards
together with their accompanying documents are issued by:

The International Accounting Standards Board (IASB) 30
Cannon Street, London, EC4M 6XH, United Kingdom. Email:
info@ifrs.org Web: www.ifrs.org

Disclaimer: The IASB, the International Financial Reporting
Standards (IFRS) Foundation, the authors and the publishers
do not accept responsibility for any loss caused by acting or
refraining from acting in reliance on the material in this
publication, whether such loss is caused by negligence or
otherwise to the maximum extent permitted by law.

Contents

Introduction to the course

Syllabus overview

This unit is about understanding and applying principles of effective credit control in an organisation. Students will require understanding of the principles of credit control in the context of relevant legislation, professional ethics and organisational policies.

Students will gain knowledge of sources of information and application of performance measures relating to liquidity, profitability and gearing will be fundamental to this unit.

Legal procedures and methods of collecting debts, as well as financial techniques used in granting and monitoring credit and debtors will need to be understood and demonstrated. An understanding of different types of discounts will also be required.

Students will learn the importance of liquidity management in credit control. Knowledge of bankruptcies and insolvencies will also be required including invoice discounting, factoring and credit insurance.

Students will be expected to demonstrate their ability in presenting advice and recommendations in professional manner, including any recommendations for write-offs and provisions.

Test specification for this unit assessment

Assessment method	Marking type	Duration of assessment
Computer based assessment	Partially computer/ partially human marked	2.5 hours

Learning outcomes	Weighting
1 Analyse relevant legislation and contract law impacting the credit control environment	15%
2 Critically analyse information from a variety of sources to assess credit risk and grant credit in compliance with organisational policies and procedures	45%
3 Evaluate a range of techniques to collect debts	15%
4 Critically evaluate credit control in line with organisational policies and procedures	15%
5 Present advice and recommendations to management on the credit control system	10%
Total	**100%**

Assessment structure

2½ hours duration

Competency is 70%

*Note that this is only a guideline as to what might come up. The format and content of each task may vary from what we have listed below.

Your assessment will consist of 7 tasks

Task	Expected content	Max marks	Chapter ref	Study complete
Task 1	**Relevant legislation and contract law impacting the credit control environment** The method of assessment can include drag and drop, gapfill and entering ticks. Coverage can include but not limited to: the components of a valid contract including how a contract can cease to be valid. The Data Protection Act can also be tested here including principles of good data practice. Calculations can include interest payable from late payment of commercial debts.	18	Legislation and credit control	

Task	Expected content	Max marks	Chapter ref	Study complete
Task 2	**Calculation of key performance indicators and applying a scoring system to reach an assessment decision recommendation** Students should anticipate having at least two years' worth of financial statements to support a credit facility application from a new or existing customer. The indicators to calculate will typically fall into three categories; profitability, liquidity and gearing. Examples can include: Net profit margin Operating profit margin Return on capital employed Current and quick ratios Inventory holding period Accounts payables collection period Accounts payable payment period Gearing ratio Interest cover Once the performance indicators have been calculated it is likely a credit rating scoring system will need to be applied to reach an assessment decision recommendation.	24	Granting credit to customers	

Task	Expected content	Max marks	Chapter ref	Study complete
Task 3	**A discussion of credit control and a written analysis of financial statements and performance indicators (written)** It is likely that this task will require a written answer and students may expect the task to split into two parts. The first part may require a discussion of particular area of credit management or control. The second part of Task 3 could require an analysis of one or more sets of customer financial statements in support of a credit application. Alternatively performance indicators may be supplied instead of financial statements. Students need to be prepared to analyse results, provide supporting explanations and reach a conclusion on whether credit can be given or extended.	30	Managing the granting of credit & Granting credit to customers	
Task 4	**Calculation of key indicators, completion of a communication analysing results along with a recommendation on whether credit should be given or extended** It is likely two or more year's customer financial statements will be supplied with a request to calculate key performance indicators. The indicators to calculate will typically fall into three categories; profitability, liquidity and gearing. Please refer to Task 2 for potential examples. The communication may be an email format and completed by data entry and picklists.	20	Granting credit to customers	

Task	Expected content	Max marks	Chapter ref	Study complete
Task 5	**Legal aspects, techniques for credit control and knowledge of aged receivables reports.** The method of assessment can include drag and drop, gapfill and entering ticks. The following techniques could be tested in this task: Identification of appropriate courts Specific clauses contained in contracts Techniques to manage credit, for example, use of factoring agencies Bankruptcy and insolvency Aged receivables reports Remedies for breach of contract	22	Legislation and credit control, Methods of credit control & Managing the supply of credit	
Task 6	**VAT aspects, liquidity management, calculation of discounts, calculation of cash flows and credit management techniques** The method of assessment can include drag and drop, gapfill and entering ticks. The following techniques could be tested in this task: Knowledge on how to deal with VAT Calculation of discount costs including the simple and compound interest methods Aspects of liquidity management Calculation of expected cash flows from customers Credit management techniques, for example credit insurance	16	Managing the granting of credit, Methods of credit control & Managing the supply of credit	

BPP
LEARNING MEDIA

Task	Expected content	Max marks	Chapter ref	Study complete
Task 7	**Review of an aged receivables report or other information identifying actions for each customer(written)** This task will require students to take into account all available information and make a written response outlining the appropriate actions to take appropriate to the individual customer's circumstances. Calculations of expected receipts from customers may also be required.	20	Managing the supply of credit	

Skills bank

Our experience of preparing students for this type of assessment suggests that to obtain competency, you will need to develop a number of key skills.

What do I need to know to do well in the assessment?

This unit is one of the optional Level 4 units. The purpose of the unit is to cover the principles of effective credit control in an organisation.

To be successful in the assessment you need to:

- Analyse legislation and contract law and its impact on credit management. In addition be able to assess credit risk and grant credit in compliance with policies and procedures.

- Evaluate credit control policies and procedures and various methods of debt collection. Additionally to be able to present advice and recommendations to management.

Assumed knowledge

Credit Management is an **optional** unit and several concepts and topics may be new to you. Some areas were covered briefly in previous units of the AAT qualification and these include:

- The legal environment
- Aged receivable reports
- Irrecoverable and allowances for doubtful debts

Assessment style

In the assessment you will complete tasks by:

1   Entering narrative by selecting from drop down menus of narrative options known as **picklists**

2   Using **drag and drop** menus to enter narrative

3   Typing in numbers, known as **gapfill** entry

4   Entering **ticks**

5   Entering **dates** by selecting from a calendar

6   **Written** answers

You must familiarise yourself with the style of the online questions and the AAT software before taking the assessment. As part of your revision, login to the **AAT website** and attempt their **online practice assessments**.

Introduction to the assessment

The question practice you do will prepare you for the format of tasks you will see in the *Credit Management* assessment. It is also useful to familiarise yourself with the introductory information you **may** be given at the start of the assessment. For example:

> You have **2 hours and 30 minutes** to complete this sample assessment.
>
> The assessment contains **7 tasks** and you should attempt to complete every task.
>
> Each task is independent. You will not need to refer to your answers to previous tasks.
>
> Read **every** task carefully to make sure you understand what is required.
>
> Where the date is relevant, it is given in the task data.
>
> Both minus signs and brackets can be used to indicate negative numbers **unless** task instructions say otherwise.
>
> You must use a full stop to indicate a decimal point. For example, write 100.57 **not** 100,57 OR 100 57.
>
> You may use a comma to indicate a number in the thousands, but you don't have to. For example, 10000 and 10,000 are both acceptable.

1   As you revise, use the **BPP Passcards** to consolidate your knowledge. They are a pocket-sized revision tool, perfect for packing in that last-minute revision.

2   Attempt as many tasks as possible in the **Question Bank**. There are plenty of assessment-style tasks which are excellent preparation for the real exam.

3   Always **check** through your own answers as you will in the real assessment, before looking at the solutions in the back of the Question Bank.

Key to icons

	Key term	A key definition which is important to be aware of for the assessment
	Formula to learn	A formula you will need to learn as it will not be provided in the assessment
	Formula provided	A formula which is provided within the assessment and generally available as a pop-up on screen
	Activity	An example which allows you to apply your knowledge to the technique covered in the Course Book. The solution is provided at the end of the chapter
	Illustration	A worked example which can be used to review and see how an assessment question could be answered
	Assessment focus point	A high priority point for the assessment
	Open book reference	Where use of an open book will be allowed for the assessment
	Real life examples	A practical real life scenario

AAT qualifications

The material in this book may support the following AAT qualifications:

AAT Professional Diploma in Accounting Level 4, AAT Professional Diploma in Accounting at SCQF Level 8 and Certificate: Accounting (Level 5 AATSA).

Supplements

From time to time we may need to publish supplementary materials to one of our titles. This can be for a variety of reasons, from a small change in the AAT unit guidance to new legislation coming into effect between editions.

You should check our supplements page regularly for anything that may affect your learning materials. All supplements are available free of charge on our supplements page on our website at:

www.bpp.com/learning-media/about/students

Improving material and removing errors

There is a constant need to update and enhance our study materials in line with both regulatory changes and new insights into the assessments.

From our team of authors BPP appoints a subject expert to update and improve these materials for each new edition.

Their updated draft is subsequently technically checked by another author and from time to time non-technically checked by a proof reader.

We are very keen to remove as many numerical errors and narrative typos as we can but given the volume of detailed information being changed in a short space of time we know that a few errors will sometimes get through our net.

We apologise in advance for any inconvenience that an error might cause. We continue to look for new ways to improve these study materials and would welcome your suggestions. Please feel free to contact our AAT Head of Programme at nisarahmed@bpp.com if you have any suggestions for us.

Managing the granting of credit

1

Learning outcomes

2.1	Explain sources of credit status and assessment methods used in granting credit
	• Extensive range of internal and external sources of information
	• External – credit agencies, references, accounts, publications and credit circles
	• Internal – records, conversations, emails, staff and meetings
	• Usefulness and appropriateness of different types of information
2.3	Present and justify reasons for granting, refusing, amending or extending credit
	• Justify organisational policies and procedures
	• Assess and communicate changes to credit
4.1	Explain the importance of liquidity management
	• The characteristics of an effective credit control system

Assessment context

On the Credit Management unit you should be prepared to identify the various sources of information when reaching a credit assessment decision and also to identify the usefulness of this information in different circumstances.

Qualification context

You may have met different sources of information on other units of the AAT qualification, however the assessment of customer credit and credit control is primarily dealt with in the Credit Management unit.

Business context

Credit management can be considered one of the most important factors in business survival. Even the most profitable of businesses may run into trouble if cash is not available to pay their debts as they fall due. An example can be when a business is unable to pay staff as money is owing to the business from debtors. Ensuring receivables pay on time helps to maintain an appropriate level of cash in the business. This is where having an effective credit management policy and credit assessment process becomes crucial.

Chapter overview

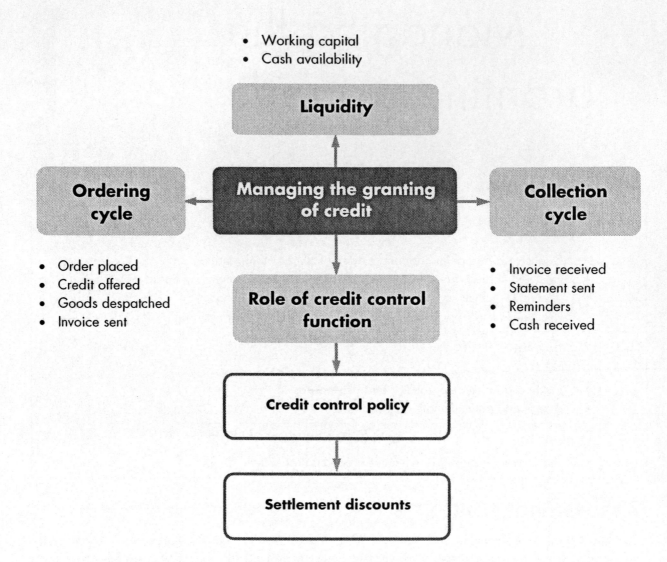

- Working capital
- Cash availability

Liquidity

Ordering cycle

Managing the granting of credit

Collection cycle

- Order placed
- Credit offered
- Goods despatched
- Invoice sent

- Invoice received
- Statement sent
- Reminders
- Cash received

Role of credit control function

Credit control policy

Settlement discounts

Introduction

Credit management is about organisations having appropriate procedures to manage the granting of credit to customers and having effective **credit control systems** to ensure that customers settle their accounts as agreed.

Having good credit management will help ensure that there will be enough cash on hand to pay obligations as they fall due. Having adequate cash, or assets that can be converted into cash, is known as **liquidity**.

Liquidity is the ability of an organisation to pay its suppliers on time, meet its operational costs such as wages and salaries and to pay longer-term outstanding amounts such as loan repayments. Adequate liquidity is often a key factor in contributing to the success or failure of a business.

Examples of liquid assets include: cash, short-term deposits, trade receivables and inventories. These component parts are called the working capital of a business.

Assessment focus point

The importance of liquidity is one of the fundamental aims of the Credit Management unit and any improvement in the credit management of an organisation will help improve the liquidity of an organisation.

Illustration 1

A company has receivables outstanding of £20,000 that it hopes to receive from customers in four weeks. In the meantime the company has an obligation to pay its own suppliers £16,000 in two weeks. The company has £10,000 in the bank and a further £10,000 available as an overdraft facility.

Clearly, the company will not have enough cash to pay the full £16,000 to suppliers in two weeks. One option open to the company would be to settle the £16,000 by £10,000 from the bank and use £6,000 from the overdraft facility; however, the use of short-term finance such as an overdraft can work out expensive. Alternative options would be to renegotiate a longer payment with suppliers or encourage customers to pay more quickly.

Activity 1: Comparing financial position

The following table shows a summary of three businesses: A, B and C.

Required

Identify which business is in the weakest financial position.

Extract from accounting records		✓
Business A	• Cash: £2,000 • Trade receivables payment expected this week: £2,500 • Rent payable today: £1,500	
Business B	• Cash: £200 • Trade receivables now overdue: £3,000 • Wages payable at end of week: £1,000	
Business C	• Cash: £1,000 • Trade receivables payment expected next week: £5,000 • Electricity bill payable in two weeks: £1,200	

1 The role of credit control

Cash and credit transactions

We must be quite clear about the distinction between transactions which are for cash and those which are on credit.

A **cash transaction** is one that takes place either with coins and notes, a cheque, a credit card or a debit card. Cash transactions are basically those for which money will be available in the business bank account almost immediately, once the amounts have been paid into the bank.

A **credit transaction** is one where the receipt or the payment is delayed for a period of time, as agreed between the two parties to the transaction. Many business sales and purchases are made on credit, whereby the goods are delivered or received now but payment is agreed to be received or made in, say, 30 or 60 days.

Granting credit

The decision as to whether or not to grant credit to customers is an important commercial decision. The granting of credit to customers means that they will be able to delay payment for goods purchased – but this delay is an important marketing aspect of business that almost always leads to a greater level of sales.

The benefit of offering credit to customers is, therefore, additional sales and accompanying profits. However, there are also costs involved in offering credit:

*   Interest cost – if money is received later from customers then the business is either losing interest, as it does not have the money in its bank account, or is being charged more interest on any overdraft balance

*   Irrecoverable debts cost – if sales are made for cash then the money is received at the time of the sale; with a credit sale there is always some risk that the goods will be despatched but never paid for

Despite these costs of granting credit, most businesses trade on a credit basis with at least some of their customers due to the benefits of additional sales and competitive advantage.

As we have seen there are two main costs involved in trading with customers on credit: the interest cost and the irrecoverable debts cost. The role of the **credit control function** is to minimise these costs.

In a small organisation the credit control function may consist of a single member of the accounting operation, but in a larger institution the credit control function may be an entire department.

There are two main stages in the credit control function:

*   The **ordering cycle**
*   The **collection cycle**

The ordering cycle

The ordering cycle can be illustrated:

Customer places
order

|

Customer credit
status established

|

Customer offered
credit

|

Goods despatched

|

Goods delivered

|

Invoice despatched

The collection cycle

The collection cycle starts where the ordering cycle finishes:

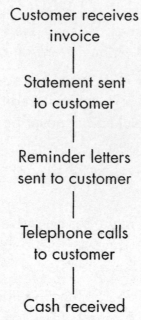

Customer receives
invoice

|

Statement sent
to customer

|

Reminder letters
sent to customer

|

Telephone calls
to customer

|

Cash received

Supply of goods and of services

A business may be supplying either goods or services to a customer. A manufacturing or wholesale organisation will be selling goods to another business, whereas a service company (such as an accountancy firm or a cleaning contractor) will be providing services. Whatever the type of company, they are likely to be offering credit to their customers.

Activity 2: The ordering cycle stages

What are the main elements of the ordering cycle for goods to be sold on credit?

2 Credit control policy

A **credit control policy** is a policy that sets out the terms and conditions when supplying goods or services on credit. Each business has its own credit control policies and procedures but all tend to cover the following areas:

- Assessment of credit standing of new customers
- Assessment of credit standing of existing customers
- Customers exceeding credit limits
- Terms and conditions of credit granted
- Payment methods allowed
- Collection procedures

Terms and conditions of credit granted

The credit terms offered to a customer are part of the agreement between the business and the customer and as such should normally be in writing. **The terms of credit** are the precise agreements with the customer as to how and when payment for the goods should be made. The most basic element of the terms of credit is the time period in which the customer should pay the invoice for the goods. There are a variety of ways of expressing these terms:

- Net 10/14/30 days – payment is due 10 or 14 or 30 days after delivery of the goods

- Weekly credit – all goods must be paid for by a specified date in the following week

- Half-monthly credit – all goods delivered in one-half of the month must be paid for by a specified date in the following half-month

- Monthly credit – all goods delivered in one month must be paid for by a specified date in the following month

Settlement and cash discounts

In some cases customers may be offered a **settlement discount** or **cash discount** for payment within a certain period which is shorter than the stated credit period.

The terms of such a settlement discount may be expressed as follows:

Net 30 days, 2% discount for payment within 14 days.

This means that the basic payment terms are that the invoice should be paid within 30 days of its date but that if payment is made within 14 days of the invoice date a 2% discount can be deducted. It is up to the customer to decide whether or not to take advantage of the settlement discount offered.

Activity 3: Settlement and cash discounts

Offering settlement discounts can have advantages and disadvantages for the business offering the discount.

Required

Identify possible advantages and disadvantages of such a policy below.

Offering settlement discounts to customers	
Advantages	Disadvantages

Activity 4: Identification of terms and conditions

If an invoice includes the term 'net monthly' what does this mean?

	✓
Invoice must be paid in the month of issue of invoice	
Invoice must be paid the month after the invoice date	
Invoice must be paid within a month of the invoice date	
Invoice must be paid net of any discount within a month of the invoice date	

Assessment focus point

In the assessment you may be asked to identify key areas of a credit control policy and give reasons or justify why the policy has specific procedures included in the policy.

Illustration 2

It is important to have procedures for accepting credit applications from new customers, as there will be no record of trading history to base a credit application decision upon. Why would it be necessary, though, to have procedures for existing customers?

Procedures for assessing the credit standing for existing customers are needed as existing customers may be looking to increase their credit limit or negotiate new terms of business regarding discounts and credit periods.

Activity 5: Policies and procedures

Explain why a credit control policy should contain procedures on customers who have exceeded their credit limits.

3 Assessment of credit status

The decision to grant credit to a customer is an extremely important commercial judgment. The granting of credit to a customer normally leads to continued and possibly increasing sales to that customer. However, there are also risks involved:

- The customer may extend the period of credit by not paying within the stated credit period and, therefore, deprive the seller of cash which may be vital for the purposes of cash flow.

- The customer may never pay at all if, for example, they went into liquidation with no money available to pay creditors.

Therefore, a very important role of the credit controller is to be able to assess the credit status of customers to determine whether or not they should be granted a period of credit, how long that credit period should be and what their credit limit should be. This role applies not only to new customers of the business but also to established customers who may wish to increase their credit limit or renegotiate their credit terms.

What is the credit controller looking for?

- Will the customer pay within stated credit terms?
- Will the customer's business remain solvent?

- Will any risk of late or non-payment be acceptable when compared to the additional sales expected?

Activity 6: Risks of granting credit

What are the risks of granting credit to a customer?

Assessment process

The process of assessing a customer's credit status, and possible actions, can be illustrated:

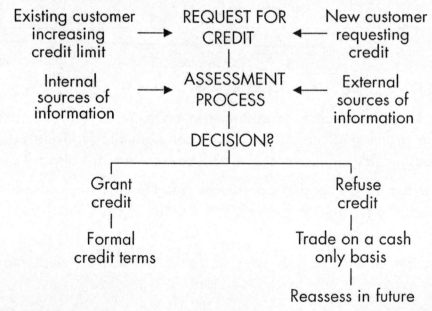

Communication of assessment decision

Once a decision has been taken to grant credit to a customer, then the details of the credit limit and terms and conditions of trading and payment will be communicated to the customer in writing. If the credit application has been refused then the reasons for the refusal will be communicated to the customer, also in writing.

4 Sources of information

When assessing the credit status of either an established or a new customer there are a variety of sources of information that the credit controller can draw upon. Some are external to the business and others are internal.

Remember that the credit controller is concerned about the customer's ability and tendency to pay within the stated credit terms and also that the customer will remain solvent. No single source of information can guarantee either of these but there are a variety of sources which can be considered; all of the information can be pooled for a final decision on credit status to be made.

The sources of information available for assessing a customer's credit status include the following:

External sources

- Bank reference
- Trade reference
- Credit reference agencies
- Credit circles (sharing of credit information between businesses)
- Companies House (for filed financial statements)
- Management accounts from the customer
- Media publications
- The internet

Internal sources

- Staff knowledge communicated by conversations, emails and meetings

- Customer visits

- Financial analysis of either external published financial statements or internal management accounts provided by the customer

- Previous trading history

Activity 7: Sources of information

Sources of credit status information can come from a variety of sources.

Required

Indicate whether each of the following sources of information for assessing the credit status of customer is internal or external.

Source	Internal or external?
Reference obtained from a credit reference agency	
Calculation of performance ratios from the customer's financial statements	
Conversations with a company's own sales team for feedback on a customer's trading reputation	
Entering a customer's name into an internet search engine	
Visiting a customer's premises when viewing or demonstrating some samples	
Reviews in a trade publication	
Analysis of an aged receivables report	

Chapter summary

- Adequate liquidity is often a key factor in contributing to the success or failure of a business. The liquidity of a business is the availability of cash or assets which can easily be converted into cash.

- The benefit of offering credit to customers is the likely increase in sales. However there are also costs of lost interest and potential irrecoverable debts. The role of the credit control function is to minimise these costs.

- The credit control function is involved in the ordering cycle in establishing customer credit status and offering credit terms and also throughout the collection cycle.

- Every business will have its own credit control policies, terms and conditions regarding how and when payment is to be made by credit customers.

- When evaluating a customer's credit status the concerns are to ensure that the customer will pay within the stated credit terms and that the business will remain solvent.

- When either a potential new customer requests credit or an existing customer requests an increase in credit limit, the credit controller will make use of internal and external information about the customer, in order to determine whether or not the request should be granted.

Keywords

- **Cash transaction:** One that takes place either with coins and notes, a cheque, a credit card or a debit card

- **Collection cycle:** The process from the sending out of the sales invoice to the receipt of cash from a customer

- **Credit control function:** The person or department responsible for minimising the interest and irrecoverable debt cost involved in trading with customers on credit

- **Credit control policy:** A policy that sets out terms and conditions when supplying goods or services on credit

- **Credit control system:** A system to ensure that customers settle their accounts as agreed and that adequate liquidity is maintained for the organisation

- **Credit transaction:** One where the receipt or the payment is delayed for a period of time, as agreed between the two parties to the transaction

- **Liquidity:** The ability of the business to pay its suppliers on time and to meet other operational costs

- **Ordering cycle:** The process from when a customer places an order to the sending out of the sales invoice

- **Settlement and cash discounts:** A discount offered for payment within a shorter period than the stated credit terms

- **Terms of credit:** The precise agreements as to how and when a customer is due to pay for goods purchased

Activity answers

Activity 1: Comparing financial position

Business B has the weakest financial position.

Business B only has £200 cash available and needs to pay wages of £1,000 by the end of the week. The trade receivable of £3,000 is already overdue and there must now be a risk that it is not going to be settled in time so that the wages can be paid. This will cause liquidity problems and Business B may have to look quickly for finance elsewhere, such as a bank loan or overdraft. This will increase finance costs of Business B. If the wages remain unpaid at the end of the week workers may withdraw their labour, which would make matters worse.

Business A is able to pay the rent liability of £1,500 out of cash available of £2,000, though the trade receivable of £2,500 needs to be monitored to ensure the money is received as expected.

Business C is expecting a receipt of £5,000 next week from trade receivables. As the electricity bill is due in two weeks this will allow the bill to be settled. However, as the electricity bill is for £1,200 and only £1,000 cash is available Business C is dependent on the £5,000 being paid. If the receipt is late Business C will also need to seek alternative finance. The expected receipt of £5,000 needs to be monitored carefully to ensure this is paid on time.

Activity 2: The ordering cycle stages

The ordering cycle involves the following:

- Customer places order
- Customer credit status established
- Customer is offered credit
- Goods are despatched
- Good are delivered
- Invoice is despatched

Activity 3: Settlement and cash discounts

Offering settlement discounts to customers	
Advantages	Disadvantages
If cash from customers is received more quickly this will improve liquidity and allow the business to reinvest in stock and pay expenses Reduces the risk of irrecoverable debts, as once a debt has been settled any risk is eliminated Provides customer satisfaction and increases goodwill	Can give a message to customers of being desperate for sales Customers may always expect discounts The financial cost of the discount itself

Activity 4: Identification of terms and conditions

	✓
Invoice must be paid in the month of issue of invoice	
Invoice must be paid the month after the invoice date	
Invoice must be paid within a month of the invoice date	✓
Invoice must be paid net of any discount within a month of the invoice date	

Activity 5: Policies and procedures

A credit control policy should contain procedures for dealing with customers who have exceeded their credit limits, so that credit control staff know the actions to take to encourage late payers to settle their accounts in a timely manner.

Activity 6: Risks of granting credit

There are two main risks in granting credit to a customer:

- The customer will exceed the stated credit period therefore depriving the seller of the use of cash.

- The customer may never pay at all – an irrevocable debt.

Activity 7: Sources of information

Source	Internal or external?
Reference obtained from a credit reference agency	external
Calculation of performance ratios from the customer's financial statements	internal
Conversations with a company's own sales team for feedback on a customer's trading reputation	internal
Entering a customer's name into an internet search engine	external
Visiting a customer's premises when viewing or demonstrating some samples	internal
Reviews in a trade publication	external
Analysis of an aged receivables report	internal

1   **Which of the following are the main costs of making sales on credit?**

(i)   Loss of customers
(ii)   Loss of interest
(iii) Loss of goodwill
(iv)   Irrecoverable debts

A   (i) and (ii)
B   (ii) and (iii)
C   (i) and (iv)
D   (ii) and (iv)

2   **Which of the following is not a main element of the collection cycle which will be part of the role of the credit control function within an organisation?**

A   Customer receives reminder letter
B   Customer receives statement
C   Customer receives invoice
D   Customer places order

3   A company sets a credit policy of normal payment within 14 days but a 3% settlement discount for payment within seven days.

How would this policy be expressed on an invoice?

4   A potential new customer approaches your business with a request for credit facilities.

Which of the following are processes that would be followed by the credit controller?

(i)   Analysis of external information
(ii)   Analysis of aged receivables listing
(iii) Analysis of payment history
(iv)   Analysis of internally produced ratios
(v)   Communication of decision to customers

A   (i), (ii), (iii), (v)
B   (ii), (iii), (iv)
C   (i), (iv), (v)
D   All of them

5   **Are credit circles an internal or external source of credit information?**

Granting credit to customers

2

Learning outcomes

2.1	Explain sources of credit status and assessment methods used in granting credit
	• Extensive range of internal and external sources of information • External – credit agencies, references, accounts, publications and credit circles • Internal – records, conversations, emails, staff and meetings • Usefulness and appropriateness of different types of information
2.2	Analyse the credit status of existing and potential customers using relevant ratios and performance indicators
	• Analyse credit scoring systems and overtrading • Calculate liquidity ratios – current, quick, receivables, payables and inventory • Calculate profitability indicators – gross profit, net profit, interest cover and return on capital employed (ROCE) • Calculate debt indicators – gearing • Calculate cash flow indicators – earnings before interest, taxes, depreciation and amortisation (EBITDA), EBITDA interest cover and EBITDA to debt • Determine the working capital cycle • Examine receivables analysis – importance and application • Calculate and interpret average periods of credit
2.3	Present and justify reasons for granting, refusing, amending or extending credit
	• Justify organisational policies and procedures • Assess and communicate changes to credit • Identify threats to objectivity that may exist when deciding whether to grant credit
5.1	Select relevant, accurate and timely information and present it effectively
	• Prepare reports with recommendations • Analyse, recommend and justify action to management for a given scenario

Assessment context

The calculation of financial ratios and the communication of assessment decisions are an extremely important part of the Credit Management unit and is very likely to appear on the assessment. Students must be able to calculate and interpret financial ratios and performance indicators correctly and present results to the required decimal places. Appropriate credit decisions can then be communicated to potential customers, based on the calculations made.

Qualification context

The calculation of financial ratios and other performance indicators can also appear in the Level 4 unit Financial Statements of Limited Companies.

Business context

Businesses that trade on credit rely on the credit control function to arrive at the correct credit assessment decision. An inappropriate credit decision can result in irrecoverable debts if customers fail to pay or loss of valuable sales from customers who have been incorrectly refused credit.

Chapter overview

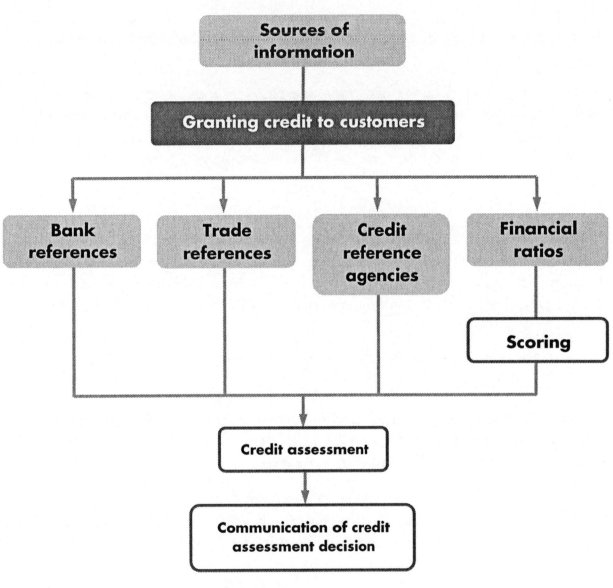

Introduction

In this chapter we consider how to evaluate the credit status of existing and new customers. This process will be undertaken by using a variety of information collected from both internal and external sources. You will need to be able to extract relevant information and to prepare calculations based upon the information provided. Once the customer's information has been assessed then the credit terms can be agreed. Alternatively, it may be necessary to refuse credit at this stage and this must be communicated to the customer.

The credit controller is concerned about the customer's ability and tendency to pay within the stated credit terms and also that the customer will remain solvent. No single source of information can guarantee either of these, but there are a variety of sources which can be considered; all of the information can be pooled for a final decision on credit status to be made.

1 External sources of information

If the credit controller wishes to assess the solvency of the customer and the likelihood of them paying within the stated credit period then two of the most obvious potential sources of information are the customer's bank and other suppliers that the customer uses.

When a new customer approaches the business with an order and a request for credit, it is normal practice for the credit controller to ask for a **bank reference** and, normally, two **trade references**. The business will make a request to the new customer for details of their bank and for details of two other suppliers with whom they regularly trade. This may be done in a letter or, more usually, by sending the customer a standard **credit application form**.

Bank references

Care needs to be taken when interpreting bank reference replies. The banks have two considerations when replying to a request for a reference regarding a customer:

- Confidentiality of the customer's affairs

- Accusations of negligence from the recipient of the reference if the reference proves to be wrong

As a consequence, bank references tend to all be worded in a similar manner with a well-known 'real' meaning. Examples of the most commonly used phrases as a reply to a request for a credit reference, and their 'real' meaning, are as follows:

Bank's reply The customer's credit for £x is:	Real meaning
Undoubted	The best type of reference – the customer should be of low risk for the figures stated
Considered good for your purposes	Probably OK and a reasonable risk but not as good as 'undoubted'
Should prove good for your figures	Not quite as certain as the other two and therefore warrants further investigation
Well-constituted business with capital seeming to be fully employed: we do not consider that the directors/owners would undertake a commitment they could not fulfil	Not very hopeful – this probably means the business has cash flow problems and credit should not be extended to them
Unable to speak for your figures	The worst – the bank seems to believe that the business is already overstretched – definitely no credit to be granted

Trade references

Once the business has received details of trade referees from the potential customer, it is standard practice to send out a letter asking for information from them. Typical information requested can include: length of time traded with, credit terms, payment record and any problems with the account.

Problems with trade references

- Some firms deliberately pay two or three suppliers promptly in order to use them as trade referees, while delaying payment to their other suppliers.

- The trade referee may be connected or influenced in some way by the potential customer. For example, it may be a business owned by one of the directors of the customer.

- The trade referee given may not be particularly strict themselves regarding credit control, therefore their replies might not be typical – the genuine nature of the trade referee should be checked.

- Even if the reference is genuine and favourable, it may be that trade with this supplier is on a much smaller basis or on different credit terms to that being sought by the customer.

Activity 1: Bank reference reply

What would be the typical response of a credit controller to a bank reference which reads 'unable to speak for your figures'?

A   Grant credit
B   Further investigation of external information
C   Do not grant credit
D   Further investigation of internal information

Activity 2: Interpreting references

You are the credit controller for a company. You have issued a standard request for bank and trade references in connection with a potential new customer and received the replies set out below.

The potential customer, Conrad Ltd, wishes to trade on credit with your company and has asked for a credit limit of £8,000 with payment terms of payment within 45 days of the invoice date.

Bank reference: Conrad Ltd

Supplied by Bourne Bank

'The customer's credit for £8,000 is considered good for your purposes.'

Trade reference: Conrad Ltd

Supplied by XYZ Ltd

How long has the customer been trading with you?   6 mths

Your credit terms with customer per month   £ 5,000

Period of credit granted   ....45 days...............

Payment record   (Prompt)/occasionally late/slow

Have you ever suspended credit to the customer?   Yes/(No)

If yes – when and for how long?...

Any other relevant information ....

....

Required

What, if any, conclusions could you draw from the above references?

Credit reference agencies

Credit reference agencies are commercial organisations which specialise in providing a variety of information regarding the credit status of companies and individuals. These agencies have large databases of information and can provide historic information such as financial reports, directors' details, payment history, any insolvency proceedings or bankruptcy orders for individuals, and bankers' opinions. They will sometimes also provide a credit rating.

Examples of credit reference agencies in the UK are Equifax, Dun & Bradstreet and Experian.

It must be borne in mind that they are a summary of only some of the information about the customer and that they may be based upon out-of-date historical data.

Credit circle

Credit circles are groups of companies which are usually competitors; this means that they tend to have customers or potential customers in common. Often such groups of companies will meet formally every few months to discuss relevant matters and also can communicate informally on a more regular basis.

Companies House

If the potential customer is a company then it must file certain financial information regarding its annual accounts and directors with Companies House. This information can be accessed by anyone but is unlikely to be particularly up-to-date, as companies need not file their annual accounts until some considerable time after their year end.

Publications and the internet

More up-to-date information can also often be found about a customer from various media sources. Newspapers such as the Financial Times run articles on many companies, as do various trade journals. The internet is a powerful tool for information and, by running a search on a company name, you may be able to find a number of useful articles and updates.

2 Internal sources of information

Internal sources of information about an existing or potential customer can include information from employees within the organisation and information that is analysed by employees. In most cases the employees of a business will have little information about potential customers but should have a good level of knowledge of existing customers. Internal sources of information can include: business records, for example payment records, internal email communications between staff and staff meetings. Staff meetings can be held on a regular basis to discuss payment patterns of customers or on an ad hoc basis to discuss one particular customer. An aged receivables analysis is an important internal report and we will look at this specific report in some depth in a later chapter.

Staff knowledge

The sales staff deal with customers on a regular basis. They are likely to have opinions as to how well a customer is doing and how efficient it is. The sales ledger staff will be able to provide information about the payment history of the customer and if it has been staying within credit limits.

Customer visits

Some internal staff, particularly the sales team, are likely to pay fairly regular visits to the customer's premises and they should be able to provide feedback as to how prosperous and efficient the customer appears to be.

3 Financial ratio analysis

The purpose of analysing the financial statements for credit control assessment is to find indicators of the customer's performance and position in four main areas:

- Profitability indicators
- Liquidity indicators
- Debt indicators
- Cash flow indicators

In general terms this analysis is only useful if it is carried out over a period of time, analysing financial statements for at least the last three years to determine any trends in business performance.

Profitability ratios

When credit has been granted one major concern will be the profitability of the customer. If the customer is not profitable in the long term then it will eventually go out of business and this may mean a loss, in the form of an irrecoverable debt, if it has been granted credit.

The main profitability ratios which will give indicators of the customer's long-term profitability are:

- Gross profit margin
- Net profit margin
- Return on capital employed
- Net asset turnover

Formula to learn

Gross profit margin

$$\frac{\text{Gross profit}}{\text{Revenue}} \times 100\%$$

This gives an indication of how profitable the trading activities of the business are. This would be expected to remain fairly constant or increase over time.

Formula to learn

Net profit margin (profit for the period)

$$\frac{\text{Net profit}}{\text{Revenue}} \times 100\%$$

The net profit (or profit for the period) is profit after all expenses have been deducted; it therefore indicates the overall profitability of the business.

The usual profit figure to use is the operating profit (or profit from operations) and therefore you could be asked for the **operating profit margin** in the assessment.

Activity 3: Gross profit and operating profit margins

A company has a revenue of £137,500. Gross profit amounts to £27,500 and, after operating expenses are deducted, operating profit amounts to £13,750.

Required

Calculate the gross profit margin percentage and operating profit margin percentage.

	%
Gross profit margin	
Operating profit margin	

Formula to learn

Return on capital employed (ROCE)

$$\frac{\text{Net profit}}{\text{Capital employed}} \times 100\%$$

This is the overall profit indicator showing the profit as a percentage of the capital employed, or the net assets of the business. This should increase or remain constant over time.

Capital employed is share capital, reserves and debt (borrowings) but can also be measured as the net asset total of the business.

If measured on the basis of net assets, then this becomes a measure of the return on equity, since debt is excluded from the calculation.

The basis for calculating capital employed should be clearly stated in your assessment, but we have included debt when calculating capital employed during the remainder of this chapter.

> **Formula to learn**
>
> **Net asset turnover**
>
> $$\frac{\text{Revenue}}{\text{Capital employed}}$$

This ratio, measured as the number of times that revenue represents capital employed (or net assets), shows the efficiency of the use of the capital employed in (or net assets of) the business and, together with the net profit margin, helps to explain any change in return on capital employed.

Activity 4: Return on capital employed

A company has a gross profit of £152,000 and operating profit of £76,000. Share capital is £200,000, reserves total £188,000 and there is a long-term loan of £100,000.

Required

Calculate the company's return on capital employed (to one decimal place).

	%
Return on capital employed	

Liquidity ratios

The purpose of calculating liquidity ratios is to provide indicators of the short-term and medium-term stability and solvency of the business. Can the business pay its debts when they fall due?

Liquidity indicators can be considered in total by the calculation of two overall liquidity ratios:

- Current ratio
- Quick ratio or acid test ratio

Liquidity and working capital management can also be examined by looking at the individual elements of the working capital of the business and calculating various turnover ratios:

- Inventory holding period (or inventory turnover)

- Accounts receivable collection period (or receivables' turnover)
- Accounts payable payment period (or payables' turnover)

Formula to learn

Current ratio

$$\frac{\text{Current assets}}{\text{Current liabilities}}$$

This is a measure of whether current assets are sufficient to pay off current liabilities. It is sometimes stated that the ideal ratio is 2:1 but this will depend upon the type of business.

In computer-based tasks you should enter the ratio as a number, entered to the specified number of decimal places if applicable. A ratio of 2:1 would be entered as 2, (since 2/1 = 2). If the ratio was 1:2 then it would be entered as 0.5 (since 1/2 = 0.5).

Activity 5: Current ratio

A company's current assets are £3,930 and current liabilities amount to £2,620.

Required

(a) Calculate the current ratio.

The company has now spent £1,530 out of the bank account and current liabilities have the remained the same.

Required

(b) Calculate a revised current ratio.

(c) What impact would your results in (a) and (b) be on your credit assessment for the company?

Formula to learn

Quick ratio/acid test ratio

$$\frac{\text{Current assets} - \text{inventory}}{\text{Current liabilities}}$$

Inventory is removed from the current assets in this measure of liquidity, as it tends to take longer to turn into cash than other current assets. It is sometimes stated that the ideal ratio is 1:1 but again this is dependent upon the type of business.

Formula to learn

Inventory holding period

$$\frac{\text{Inventory}}{\text{Cost of sales}} \times 365 \text{ days}$$

The inventory holding period (sometimes called inventory turnover) measures how many days, on average, inventory is held before it is sold. This will depend upon the type of inventory but should ideally not increase significantly over time.

Formula to learn

Accounts receivable collection period

$$\frac{\text{Trade receivables}}{\text{Sales}} \times 365 \text{ days}$$

This measures how many days, on average, it takes for receivables to pay and is sometimes also referred to as receivables' turnover and shows the average period of credit taken by customers. This will depend upon the type of business and the credit terms that are offered. Ideally, it should be around the average credit period offered to credit customers and similar to the time taken to pay suppliers.

Formula to learn

Accounts payable payment period

$$\frac{\text{Trade payables}}{\text{Purchases}} \times 365 \text{ days}$$

The accounts payable payment period (sometimes called payables' turnover) measures how many days, on average, the business takes to pay its trade payables. This is of direct relevance as it will give an indication of how long a period of credit the business normally takes from its suppliers.

Very often the purchases figure is not available from the financial statements and consequently **cost of sales** must be used as an approximation.

Working capital cycle

The **working capital cycle** or operating cycle measures the period of time from when cash is paid out for raw materials until the time cash is received in from customers for goods sold.

(1) A firm buys raw materials, probably on credit.

(2) It holds the raw materials for some time in stores before they are issued to the production department and turned into finished goods.

(3) The finished goods may be kept in a warehouse for some time before they are eventually sold to customers.

(4) By this time, the firm will probably have paid for the raw materials purchased.

(5) If customers buy the goods on credit, it will be some time before the cash from the sales is eventually received.

The working capital cycle or operating cycle of a business in days is calculated as:

	Days
Inventory holding period	X
Accounts receivable collection period	X
	X
Less accounts payable payment period	(X)
Working capital cycle	X

Activity 6: Working capital cycle

(a) A company has sales of £980,000 and cost of sales of £686,000. Inventory at the year end is £77,000, trade receivables are £130,000 and trade payables are £89,000.

Required

Complete the table below by calculating the indicators below to the nearest day.

	Days
Inventory holding period	
Accounts receivable collection period	
Accounts payable payment period	

(b) **Using your results in (a) above, how long is the working capital cycle?**

Gearing ratios

When assessing a customer's credit status the credit controller will also be concerned with the longer-term stability of the business. One area of anxiety here is the amount of debt in the business's capital structure and its ability to service this debt by paying the periodic interest charges.

The main measures are:

- Gearing ratio
- Interest cover

When looking at the total debt of the business, the company may also analyse debt into that payable in the short term and that payable in the long term. The short-term debt ratio can help assess what proportion of total debt is payable sooner rather than later.

> **Formula to learn**
>
> **Gearing ratio**
>
> $$\frac{\text{Total debt}}{\text{Capital employed}} \times 100\%$$

The gearing ratio is a measure of the proportion of interest-bearing debt to the total capital of the business. Debt may be referred to in the assessment as 'borrowing' or 'loans' when it is included in the statement of financial position. The capital employed for use in the gearing calculation (or total capital of the business) is usually defined as total debt plus equity. In the current financial situation, many businesses rely on a bank overdraft to keep trading. Therefore the total debt figure increasingly includes the bank overdraft figure, if the financial statements show that this is an ongoing source of finance. However, sometimes the figure used for capital employed is just the total equity (ie excluding the total debt).

The gearing ratio is often stated as ideal at 50% or less, although this will again vary between different industries and different businesses. The higher the figure the more risky the company may appear to be.

Assessment focus point

In the assessment look out for information whether debt needs to include both long-term and short-term debt. If the company is continually using an overdraft as a form of finance then this may need to be included in the total debt used by the business.

Formula to learn

Interest cover

$$\frac{\text{Profit before interest}}{\text{Interest payable}}$$

The interest cover is calculated as the number of times that the interest could have been paid; it represents the margin of safety between the profits earned and the interest that must be paid to service the debt capital. Interest cover can also be a good indicator of the profitability of a business.

Cash flow indicators

In most of the calculations so far, the profit before interest figure from the statement of profit or loss (income statement) has been used in order to calculate various ratios. However, there are many users of accounts who believe that this figure is subject to management and accounting policies, so a further figure of **EBITDA** is often used in calculations. This is earnings before interest, tax, depreciation and amortisation and means taking the earnings before profit and tax figure, and then adding back any interest and depreciation and amortisation charges.

It is argued that using this figure removes the subjective figures of depreciation and amortisation from the profit figure and gives a closer approximation to the underlying cash flows. This figure can then be used to calculate a number of further ratios which can be useful in assessing the cash flow situation of a business.

Formula to learn

EBITDA interest cover

$$\frac{\text{EBITDA}}{\text{Interest payable}}$$

This is the same calculation as for interest cover but using EBITDA instead of profit before interest.

Formula to learn

EBITDA to total debt

$$\frac{\text{EBITDA}}{\text{Total debt}} \times 100\%$$

This is a measure of the profits/cash flows available in comparison with the total debt of the company. It can give an indication of the ease with which the company can service its debt commitments from operations.

Activity 7: Cash flow indicators

A company has share capital of £200,000, reserves totalling £188,000 and a loan of £100,000. The net profit for the year is £45,000, after deducting depreciation of £12,000 and interest of £6,000.

Required

Calculate the company's gearing ratio, interest cover and EBITDA-based interest cover (to one decimal place).

Workings		
Gearing ratio (%)		
Interest cover		
EBITDA-based interest cover		

Assessment focus point

When calculating percentages always remember to multiply by 100. For example, if calculating 50 out of 200 the calculation is 50/200 × 100 = 25% and not 0.25.

Also be careful to follow rounding requirements. For example, if in the assessment you are asked to round to two decimal places then 26.174% would become 26.17% and 26.176% would become 26.18%. By convention when a figure ends in a '5' this is rounded up. For example, 26.175% would also become 26.18% when presented to two decimal places.

4 Preparing a credit assessment report and recommendation

There are a number of internal and external sources of information available to the credit controller in his attempt to assess the current credit status of an existing or potential customer. It is likely that the credit controller will review most, if not all, of these sources of information and then use the information gathered to make a decision about the customer's credit status.

This may be a clear-cut judgement where the bank reference is favourable, the trade references are sound and the analysis of the financial statements indicates a profitable and liquid business. Such a business would appear to be low risk and should be granted credit.

At the other end of the scale the bank and trade references may be unsatisfactory and an assessment of the financial statements may indicate problems with profitability and liquidity. This is a high-risk business and trade should probably only be carried out on a cash basis. In many scenarios the situation may not be clear cut and the credit controller must assess conflicting information to determine the best course of action.

Assessment focus point

In the assessment you may need to reach a credit assessment decision and justify how you reached your decision. In written answers it can be useful to state the financial ratios calculated, explain whether results are improving or deteriorating and provide possible reasons why ratios are changing and highlight any potential problems regarding profitability, liquidity or gearing.

Activity 8: Making a credit assessment decision

Your name is Tom Hunt, the credit controller at SC Fuel and Glass, and you are considering the request for £15,000 a month of credit facilities for Haven Engineering Ltd. The following references and financial statements have now been received:

Bank reference

Haven Engineering Ltd – should prove good for your figures.

Trade reference 1

Payment occasionally late and have suspended credit in the past.

Trade reference 2

Payment occasionally late and credit never suspended.

Summarised financial statements for the three years ending 31 December 20X6, 20X7 and 20X8.

Summarised statements of profit or loss

	Year ending 31 December		
	20X6 £000	20X7 £000	20X8 £000
Sales revenue	3,150	3,220	3,330
Cost of sales	(2,048)	(2,061)	(2,115)
Gross profit	1,102	1,159	1,215
Operating expenses	(645)	(676)	(732)
Operating profit	457	483	483
Finance costs	(95)	(100)	(120)
Profit before taxation	362	383	363
Taxation	(91)	(96)	(91)
Profit for the year, after taxation	271	287	272

Summarised statements of financial position

	As at 31 December		
	20X6 £000	20X7 £000	20X8 £000
Assets			
Non-current assets	3,339	3,727	4,112
Current assets			
Inventory	292	328	353
Receivables	639	670	684
Cash at bank	2	2	2
	933	1,000	1,039
Total assets	4,272	4,727	5,151
Equity and liabilities			
Equity			
Ordinary share capital	1,000	1,000	1,000
Retained earnings	1,020	1,307	1,579
Total equity	2,020	2,307	2,579
Non-current liabilities			
Borrowing	1,600	1,800	2,000
Current liabilities			
Trade payables	494	474	463
Other liabilities	158	146	109
	652	620	572
Total liabilities	2,252	2,420	2,572
Total equity and liabilities	4,272	4,727	5,151

The borrowings are long-term loans. Finance costs consists of interest payable.

Required

In your role as credit controller assess the information available regarding Haven Engineering Ltd.

Overtrading

When assessing the financial health of a business, including prospective customers, one thing to be mindful of is the possibility that the business could be **overtrading**.

Overtrading occurs when a business takes on a high volume of work and attempts to complete it, but discovers it does not have the required level of resources to do so. It may be that the business needs more employees, working capital (including cash) or assets than are available to it.

Overtrading is common when a business is just starting out and when a company is growing very rapidly (too rapidly and taking on too much new business). The business finds itself having to pay a lot of cash (eg to buy inventory, pay wages and pay the rent) before collecting cash from customers, since the customers have been allowed a period of credit (and in any case customers are not guaranteed to pay on time). As a result the business can run short of cash and may not be able to continue to pay its liabilities as they fall due.

There are a number of signs of overtrading, including:

- Rapidly increasing sales revenue as a result of offering increased periods of credit to customers, or offering credit to less creditworthy customers

- Increasing receivables and inventory levels, indicating more funds tied up and not readily converted to cash

- An overdraft for the first time, or an increase in an existing overdraft or other short-term debt that has been required to meet cash shortages

- Payables have increased, as the business has been forced to take longer to pay suppliers

- Reduced margins may be apparent if prices are discounted to grow revenue

It is important to note that the above signs may not necessarily mean there is an overtrading problem with a business, especially if there is only one of the signs present. As always it is important that a number of indicators are considered together. However, if a number of the signs are present for a particular business, the possibility of overtrading should be taken into account when deciding whether to offer credit.

Illustration 1

The financial statements of ABC Ltd have been analysed and the following information is available:

	20X8	20X7
Gross profit margin	45%	36%
Inventory holding period	63 days	55 days
Accounts receivable collection period	57 days	45 days
Gearing ratio	65%	47%

Conclusion:

The gross profit margin has increased from 36% to 45%, showing an apparently healthy increase. However the inventory holding period and the accounts receivable collection period have both increased. This means that money is tied up in inventory for longer before being turned into cash and that it is taking longer to collect money from customers.

It could be that customers are being offered more generous credit terms to encourage them to buy more, but it could also mean that ABC Ltd is selling to new customers who are taking longer to pay. Finally, the gearing ratio shows a large increase over the previous period. It could be that ABC Ltd is borrowing more, in order to invest in new assets to expand the business. Alternatively, the company may be borrowing more to cover reduced cash flow from holding inventories longer and customers taking longer to pay. The signs are that ABC Ltd could be overtrading but further investigation is needed.

5 Credit scoring

Credit scoring is a method of assessing the creditworthiness of an individual or organisation using statistical analysis and is used by organisations such as banks, utility companies, insurance companies and landlords to assess the ability of an individual or organisation to repay any loans or pay for services or goods.

Information is entered into a scoring system, and a credit score is then calculated by weighting the information. Using the credit score, lenders can predict with some accuracy how likely the borrower is to repay a debt and make payments on time.

Leading credit reference agencies use data from multiple sources to create a comprehensive, weighted score. Typically they will consider:

- Financials – profitability, liquidity/solvency, gearing, any late filing of accounts or other statutory documents

- Business details – age, size, industry, number of employees

- Publicly available data – County Court Judgements, mortgages and charges

- Payment record – payment trends, volatility, % of debts paid promptly or beyond terms

- Owners – number, experience, track record

- Economic index – risk and expectations relating to the specific industry under different economic conditions

A business that can demonstrate timely payment of its obligations, assets which easily outweigh its liabilities, a large amount of available credit and one that is not too highly geared will be deemed low risk.

Late payments and high gearing will damage the score and any insolvency/bankruptcy, judgements and foreclosure will almost certainly guarantee a failing grade.

The following credit rating (scoring) system table can be used to assess the risk of default by calculating key indicators (ratios), comparing them to the table and calculating an aggregate score.

Credit rating (scoring) system	Score
Operating profit margin	
Losses	–5
Less than 5%	0
5% and above but less than 10%	5
10% and above but less than 20%	10
More than 20%	20
Interest cover	
No cover	–30
Less than 1	–20
More than 1 but less than 2	–10
More than 2 but less than 4	0
More than 4	10
Liquidity ratio	
Less than 1	–20
Between 1 and 1.25	–10
Between 1.26 and 1.5	0
Above 1.5	10
Gearing (total debt/(total debt plus equity))	
Less than 25%	20
25% and above but less than 50%	10
More than 50% but less than 65%	0
More than 65% but less than 75%	–20
More than 75% but less than 80%	–40
More than 80%	–100
Risk	**Aggregate score**
Very low risk	Between 60 and 21
Low risk	Between 20 and 1
Medium risk	Between 0 and –24
High risk	Between –25 and –50
Very high risk	Less than –50

Activity 9: Scoring of financial ratios

Your business uses a scoring system to rate potential new customers and ahead of an assessment decision of a potential customer you have obtained a number of key financial ratios for two years' results.

Only customers who are considered to be medium risk are offered a credit facility.

Required

Using the credit rating system shown on the previous page score the following financial ratios and tick whether the application would be rejected or accepted for both years.

ABC Ltd	20X6		20X5	
	Ratio	Rating	Ratio	Rating
Operating profit margin	7%		11%	
Interest cover	1.4		0.8	
Liquidity (current) ratio	1.7		1.4	
Gearing	70%		55%	
Total credit rating				
		✓		✓
Reject credit application				
Accept credit application				

6 Communication of a credit assessment decision

Once a decision has been taken to grant credit to a customer, then the precise details of the credit limit and all terms and conditions of trading and payment must be communicated to the new customer in writing. Before this is done the credit limit must be set for the customer. When determining this, communication with the sales department will be useful to establish the expected level of orders from this customer. For example, if the sales department expects the customer to order £4,000 of goods per week and the credit terms are 30 days then a credit limit of, say, £10,000 would seriously limit the sales to this customer.

Opening a new customer account

Once a decision has been made to grant credit to a customer then a file and an account in the trade receivables ledger must be set up. For this to take place the following information will be required:

- The business name of the customer
- The contact name and title within the customer's business
- Business address and telephone number
- The credit limit agreed upon
- The payment terms agreed
- Any other terms, such as settlement discounts offered

Refusal of credit

In some cases, the credit controller may decide that it is not possible to trade with a new potential customer on credit terms.

Refusing to grant credit to a new customer is a big decision for the credit controller, as the business will not wish to lose this potential customer's business – but the credit controller will have taken a view that the risk of non-payment is too high for credit terms to be granted.

Refusal of credit does not necessarily mean that the potential customer's business is bad or is likely not to survive; it simply means that, on the evidence available to the credit controller, the chance of non-payment is too high for the company to take the risk.

There are a variety of reasons why a decision might be made not to grant credit to a new customer and could include the following:

- A non-committal or poor bank reference

- Poor trade references

- Concerns about the validity of any trade references submitted

- Adverse press comment about the potential customer

- Poor credit agency report

- Information from a member of the business's credit circle

- Indications of business weakness from analysis of the financial statements

- Lack of historical financial statements available, due to being a recently started company

The credit controller will consider all of the evidence available about a potential customer and the reason for the refusal of credit may be due to a single factor noted above or a combination of factors.

Communication of changes or refusal of credit

If a credit facility is to be changed or not granted to a potential customer then this must be communicated in a tactful and diplomatic manner. The reasons for the change or refusal of credit must be politely explained and any future actions required from the potential customer should also be made quite clear. The credit controller, while not wishing to grant credit to the customer at the current time, will also not necessarily want to lose their potential business.

In almost all cases where credit is to be refused to a potential customer the company should make it quite clear that they would be happy to trade with the customer on cash terms.

In some situations, although the granting of credit to the new customer has currently been refused, it may be that the credit controller wishes to encourage the customer to apply for credit terms in the future. For example, with a newly formed company, there may be little external information available on which the credit controller can rely at the present time – but if financial statements and references can be provided in the future then the decision as to whether or not to trade on credit terms can be re-assessed.

Communication method

In most cases it is usually expedient to communicate the reasons for the refusal of credit initially in a letter. In the letter the credit controller may suggest that a telephone call may be appropriate in order to discuss the matter and any future actions that may be necessary.

Illustration 2

Glowform Ltd has requested to trade with the SC Fuel and Glass on credit and would like a £5,000 credit limit and 60 days' credit. Tom, the credit controller requested two trade references, a bank reference and financial statements for the last three years. Glowform Ltd has provided a bank reference which states that the 'the company appears to be well constituted but we cannot necessarily speak for your figures due to the length of time that the company has been in operation'. The company has also provided one trade reference which is satisfactory from a company which allows Glowform Ltd £3,000 of credit on 30-day terms. However Glowform Ltd has only been in operation for just over a year and has, as yet, not been able to provide any financial statements.

An example of a refusal letter:

SC FUEL AND GLASS
CRAWLEY RD
CRAWLEY
CR7 JN9
Tel: 01453 732166 Fax: 01453 732177

Finance Director
Glowform Ltd

Date:

Dear Sir

Re: Request for credit facilities

Thank you for your enquiry regarding the provision of credit facilities of £5,000 of credit on 60-day terms. We have taken up your trade and bank references of which you kindly sent details.

We have some concerns about offering credit at this early stage of your business as there are as yet no financial statements for your business that we can examine. Therefore at this stage I am unable to confirm that we can provide you with credit facilities immediately.

We would, of course, be delighted to trade with you on cash terms until we have had an opportunity to examine your first year's trading figures. Therefore please send us a copy of your first year financial statements when they are available and, in the meantime, contact us if you would like to start trading on a cash basis.

Thank you for your interest in our company.

Yours faithfully

Tom Hunt
Credit controller

Activity 10: Refusal of credit reasons

What potential reasons could there be for not agreeing to trade on credit with a new customer?

Activity 11: Signs of overtrading

Identify six signs that may indicate a business is overtrading.

The ethical principle of objectivity

The AAT Code of Professional Ethics defines objectivity as an obligation not to compromise professional or business judgement because of bias, conflict of interest or undue influence of others (Association of Accounting Technicians, 2014).

This means that the credit controller will need to reach credit assessment decisions using their organisation's credit control policy and a customer's merit without any risk to objectivity.

There are a number of potential threats to objectivity and these are:

Threat	Explanation	Example
Self-interest	Financial or other interests that may influence a decision	A credit controller has shares in the company requesting credit
Self-review	A previous decision re-evaluated by the person responsible for the original decision	A junior member of a credit control team checking their own work instead of a senior credit controller
Advocacy	A person promotes a decision to the point that objectivity is compromised	Where a credit controller is biased in advocating a specific credit assessment decision
Familiarity	Due to a close personal relationship a person becomes too sympathetic to the interests of others	The spouse of a credit controller is the managing director of a company requesting credit
Intimidation	A person may be deterred from acting objectively by threats (actual or perceived)	A credit controller receiving rude and threatening telephone calls from a customer

Activity 12: Identification of threats to objectivity

A brother and sister work at the same company. The sister is a member of the sales team and her brother is the company's credit controller. The brother is paid on a fixed salary basis and the sister is remunerated on the value of sales made.

Required

What two threats to objectivity are most likely here for the management of credit?

	✓
Self-interest	
Self-review	
Advocacy	
Familiarity	
Intimidation	

Chapter summary

- When evaluating a customer's credit status the concerns will be whether the customer will pay within the stated credit terms and that the business will remain solvent.

- When either a potential new customer requests credit or an existing customer requests an increase in credit limit, the credit controller will make use of internal and external information in order to determine whether or not the request should be granted.

- External sources of information are most commonly a bank reference and two trade references.

- In some cases a credit controller will use the services of a credit reference agency for information about a potential customer and a possible credit rating or, rather more informally, from any credit circle that they may belong to.

- Other sources of external information are Companies House records, official publications and the internet.

- When considering requests from existing customers it is likely that staff within the business will have internal information about the customer and may possibly have made visits to the customer's premises.

- The most common form of internal analysis of both existing and potential new customers is financial ratio analysis of their financial accounts, preferably for the last three years or more.

- Once all of the relevant information has been gathered about a customer then a decision must be made as to whether or not to grant them credit – in many cases the information may be conflicting, with some sources suggesting that credit should be granted and other sources not proving so favourable.

- Credit scoring is a method used by organisations such as banks and utility companies to assess the creditworthiness of an individual or organisation.

- Once a decision has been made as to whether or not to grant credit to a customer, this decision must be communicated to the customer, normally in writing.

- Where credit is to be granted to a new customer, the details of the credit limit and terms of payment must be made quite clear and a new account for that customer must be opened within the trade receivables ledger.

- In some cases it may be decided to refuse credit to a customer, in which case this must be communicated in a tactful and diplomatic manner.

- In some cases a customer may be offered a chance for future re-assessment of their credit status; in the meantime an offer for trading on cash terms would be made.

Keywords

- **Accounts payable payment period:** How many days on average a business takes to pay its trade payables

- **Accounts receivable collection period:** How many days on average its takes for receivables to pay

- **Bank reference:** A bank's opinion of its customer's business position and credit status

- **Capital employed:** Share capital, reserves and debt (borrowing); also alternatively measured as the net asset total of the business

- **Credit application form:** A form sent to a prospective new customer asking for details including bank and trade reference details

- **Credit circles:** Groups of companies which can provide mutual information on current and prospective customers and their credit records

- **Credit reference agency:** A commercial organisation providing background information and credit status information about companies and individuals

- **Current ratio:** Current assets compared to current liabilities expressed as a ratio

- **Gross profit margin:** Measure of the profit from trading activities compared with revenue

- **Inventory holding period:** The average number of days for which inventory is held

- **Net asset turnover:** Measure of the amount of revenue compared with total capital employed

- **Net profit margin** (operating profit margin): Measure of the overall (operating) profit compared with revenue

- **Objectivity:** A fundamental ethical principle that avoids bias, conflict of interest or undue influence in decision making

- **Quick ratio/acid test ratio:** Current assets minus inventory as a ratio to current liabilities

- **Return on capital employed (ROCE):** Measure of the overall profit compared with total capital employed

- **Trade reference:** A reference from one of a business's current suppliers regarding its payment record

- **Working capital cycle:** Inventory holding period (days) plus accounts receivable collection period (days) less accounts payable payment period (days)

Activity 1: Bank reference reply

C   Do not grant credit

Activity 2: Interpreting references

The information in the bank reference looks positive. It is not as good as 'undoubted' but suggests that the customer is probably okay and a reasonable risk.

The trade reference looks fairly positive in that XYZ Ltd offers 45-day payment terms and receives prompt payment, which gives some confidence. However the amount of credit they offer is only £5,000 whereas Conrad Ltd has applied to you for credit of £8,000.

In conjunction with another trade reference and satisfactory other internal and external information about Conrad Ltd, a decision may be taken to grant Conrad's credit request.

Activity 3: Gross profit and operating profit margins

	%
Gross profit margin	20
Operating profit margin	10

Gross profit margin: (27,500/137,500) × 100 = 20%

Operating profit margin: (13,750/137,500) × 100 = 10%

Activity 4: Return on capital employed

	%
Return on capital employed	15.6

Return on capital employed: (76,000/488,000) × 100 = 15.6%

Activity 5: Current ratio

(a)   3,930/2,620 = 1.5:1 or 1.5

(b)   (3,930 – 1,530)/2,620 = 0.92:1 or 0.92

(c)   In part (a) the company's current assets exceed the current liabilities, therefore the company has a degree of liquidity. For every £1 of current liabilities there is £1.50 to cover those obligations. In part (b) the current assets have dropped below the current liabilities, due to money being spent out of the bank account. This could mean that the company could struggle to pay debts as they fall, including suppliers, wages and salaries, overheads and taxation. This would be a negative factor when completing a credit assessment on the company.

Activity 6: Working capital cycle

	Days
Inventory holding period	41
Accounts receivable collection period	48
Accounts payable payment period	47

Inventory holding period: (77,000/686,000) × 365 = 41 days

Accounts receivable collection period: (130,000/980,000) × 365 = 48 days

Accounts payable payment period: (89,000/686,000) × 365 = 47 days

Working capital cycle: (41 + 48 – 47) = 42 days

Activity 7: Cash flow indicators

	Workings	
Gearing ratio (%)	100,000/(200,000 + 188,000 + 100,000)	20.5%
Interest cover	(45,000 + 6,000)/6,000	8.5 times
EBITDA based interest cover	(45,000 + 6,000 + 12,000)/6,000	10.5 times

Activity 8: Making a credit assessment decision

Bank reference

The bank reference is not the most positive that might have been given and indicates that consideration should be given, in particular, to the liquidity and profitability of the company.

Trade references

Both trade references indicate that Haven Engineering Ltd is a slow payer; again, consideration should be given to information in the financial statements to try to determine whether this is due to liquidity problems, general inefficiency or a determined policy of the company. One trade reference has confirmed that credit has been suspended at least once.

Financial statement analysis

	20X6	20X7	20X8
Financial ratios:			
Profitability			
Gross profit margin	35%	36%	36.5%
Operating profit margin	14.5%	15%	14.5%
Return on capital employed	12.6%	11.8%	10.5%
Asset turnover	0.87	0.78	0.73
Liquidity			
Current ratio	1.43:1	1.61:1	1.82:1
Quick ratio	0.98:1	1.08:1	1.20:1
Inventory holding period	52 days	58 days	61 days
Accounts receivable collection period	74 days	76 days	75 days
Accounts payable payment period	88 days	84 days	80 days
Gearing			
Gearing ratio	44%	44%	44%
Interest cover	4.8 times	4.8 times	4.0 times

From the analysis of the financial ratios a number of points can be made about Haven Engineering Ltd.

Profitability

In terms of profitability, the gross profit margin has increased in each of the three years, although the operating (or net) profit margin is fairly constant.

Return on capital employed has fallen over the three years, due to the decrease in net asset turnover. There has clearly been large investment in non-current assets over the period and, as yet, this does not appear to have led to significantly increased revenue or profits.

Liquidity

The current ratio could be said to be rather low; however, it has been increasing in each of the three years, and the quick ratio appears healthy and is also improving. The inventory holding period is quite high and has increased by nine days over the period; consequently there is considerable capital tied up in the inventory holdings.

Perhaps of more concern are the accounts receivable collection period and the accounts payable payment period. The accounts receivable collection period has remained fairly constant but, at around 75 days, is a long time. This might account for the length of time that Haven Engineering Ltd takes to pay its own suppliers which, although improving, still stands at 80 days – which is 50 days longer than SC's credit terms of 30 days.

Gearing

Although there have been small increases annually in the amount of long-term loans, the gearing level has remained constant at 44%. Interest cover is also healthy at four times or over.

Recommendation

The evidence received from the bank reference, trade references and the financial statements would indicate a problem with Haven Engineering regarding the period of time which they take before paying their suppliers. The company appears to be profitable and despite the length of time their own customers take to pay, there would not appear to be too serious a liquidity problem. Therefore the late paying of suppliers could be a deliberate policy.

It is recommended that only £10,000 of credit is initially granted to Haven Engineering Ltd, with an agreement that payment is to be strictly to 30 days of the invoice date. This period of credit should perhaps be limited to a six-month period, during which the receipts from Haven Engineering Ltd should be monitored closely. Haven Engineering Ltd should be made aware that if payments are not received promptly, credit facilities will be withdrawn and only cash trading will be available.

Activity 9: Scoring of financial ratios

ABC Ltd	20X6		20X5	
	Ratio	Rating	Ratio	Rating
Operating profit margin	7%	5	11%	10
Interest cover	1.4	−10	0.8	−20
Liquidity (current) ratio	1.7	10	1.4	0
Gearing	70%	−20	55%	0
Total credit rating		−15		−10
		✓		✓
Reject credit application				
Accept credit application		✓		✓

Both years' scores fall between 0 and −24 and meet the requirement to be a medium-risk customer. On this basis the credit application would be successful and accepted.

Activity 10: Refusal of credit reasons

Reasons for not agreeing to trade on credit with a customer might include the following:

- A non-committal or unsatisfactory bank reference
- Poor trade references
- Concerns about the validity of any trade references submitted
- Adverse press comment about the potential customer
- Information from a member of the business's credit circle
- Poor credit agency report
- Indications of business weakness from analysis of financial statements
- Lack of historical financial statements available, due to being a recently started company

Activity 11: Signs of overtrading

The following factors can indicate that a business is overtrading.

1. Revenue increasing significantly in a short time period
2. Increase in inventory levels
3. Increases in trade receivables
4. Working on unsustainable low profit margins to attract trade
5. Reduction in cash balances
6. Continual use of short-term finance, for example overdrafts, to meet working capital requirements

Activity 12: Identification of threats to objectivity

	✓
Self-interest	✓
Self-review	
Advocacy	
Familiarity	✓
Intimidation	

1 You are the credit controller for AKA Ltd and you are considering a request from Kelvin & Sons which wishes to trade on credit with your company. You are considering offering a credit limit of £10,000 with payment terms of payment within 30 days of the invoice date.

You have written to Kelvin & Sons' bank, Southern Bank, asking for a reference having specified that you are considering a credit limit of £10,000. The bank's reply is given below.

'Should prove good for your figures'

What, if any, conclusions can you draw from the bank reference?

A Credit should be granted

B Credit should not be granted

C Credit should be granted if further information is positive

D No conclusion can be drawn

2 You are the credit controller for a company and you are considering a request from Caterham Ltd which wishes to trade on credit with your company. Caterham Ltd asked for a credit limit of £15,000, with terms of payment within 30 days of the invoice date. You have a standard form for trade references and Caterham Ltd has provided you with the name and address of another of its suppliers, SK Traders, to which you have sent the standard trade reference form. The reply you receive is given below.

Trade reference

We have received a request for credit from Caterham Ltd which has quoted yourselves as a referee. We would be grateful if you could answer the following questions and return this in the stamped addressed envelope enclosed.

How long has the customer been trading with you?	..4.. years . 2... mths
Your credit terms with customer per month	£ 8,000
Period of credit granted	.... 30 days...............
Payment record	Prompt/(occasionally late)/slow
Have you ever suspended credit to the customer?	Yes/(No)
If yes – when and for how long?..	
Any other relevant information	
....	

Thank you for your assistance.

What, if any, conclusions could you draw from the trade reference?

3 **What services does a credit reference agency typically provide?**

4 **Which of the following information could be provided by Companies House about a company that was requesting credit from your business?**

  A   Management accounts
  B   Directors' contracts
  C   Annual financial statements
  D   Loan agreements

5 You are the credit controller for a business and you have been approached by Franklin Ltd, which wishes to place an order with your business and to trade on credit. It would like a credit limit of £5,000 per month. Franklin Ltd has provided you with its last two years' statements of profit or loss and statements of financial position.

Statements of profit or loss for the year ended 31 March

	20X9 £000	20X8 £000
Sales revenue	1,000	940
Cost of sales	(780)	(740)
Gross profit	220	200
Operating expenses	(100)	(90)
Operating profit	120	110
Interest payable	(30)	(20)
Profit before tax	90	90
Taxation	(23)	(43)
Profit after tax	67	47

Statements of financial position at 31 March

	20X9 £000	20X8 £000
Assets		
Non-current assets	1,335	1,199
Current assets		
Inventory	110	90
Receivables	140	150
	250	240
Total assets	1,585	1,439
Equity and liabilities		
Equity		
Share capital	800	800
Retained earnings	325	278
Total equity	1,125	1,078
Current liabilities		
Trade payables	160	161
Bank overdraft	300	200
Total liabilities	460	361
Total equity and liabilities	1,585	1,439

Complete the table below by calculating the ratios given (to 2dp).

	20X9	20X8
Gross profit margin (%)		
Operating profit margin (%)		
Current ratio		
Quick ratio		
Accounts payable payment period (days)		
Interest cover (times)		

6   You are the credit manager for Acorn Enterprises and your name is Jo Wilkie. You
     have been assessing the financial statements for Little Partners, which has requested
     £8,000 of credit on 60-day terms. You also have received a satisfactory bank
     reference and trade references.

     Your analysis of the 20X7 and 20X8 financial statements shows the following
     picture:

	20X8	20X7
Gross profit margin	30%	28%
Net profit margin	4%	3%
Interest cover	1.5 times	0.9 times
Current ratio	1.3 times	0.8 times

     You are to draft a suitable letter to Little Partners, dealing with its request for credit
     facilities.

7   You are the credit controller for a business and you received a request from Dawn
     Ltd for credit of £5,000 from your company on a 30-day basis. Two trade
     references have been provided, but no bank reference. You have also been
     provided with the last set of published financial statements, which include the
     previous year's comparative figures. The trade references appeared satisfactory –
     although one is from Johannesson Partners and it has been noted that the managing
     director of Dawn Ltd is Mr F Johannesson. Analysis of the financial statements has
     indicated a decrease in profitability during the last year, a high level of gearing and
     low liquidity ratios.

     Draft a letter to the finance director of Dawn Ltd on the basis that credit is to be
     currently refused, but may be extended once the most recent financial statements
     have been examined.

Legislation and credit control

3

Learning outcomes

1.1	Examine how the main features of statute and contract law apply to credit control
	• Essential features and terminology of contract law: offer, acceptance, intention, consideration, capacity and consent
	• Legislation relating to trade descriptions – understanding including offences and breaches
	• Legislation relating to unfair contract terms – understanding, in particular, unfair terms
	• Legislation relating to sale and supply of goods and services – main terms
	• Legislation relating to consumer credit – understanding of principal terms.
1.2	Discuss remedies for breach of contract and the circumstances in which they can be used effectively
	• Express terms, implied terms, conditions, warranties, damages, specific performance, quantum meruit and action for the price
	• Statutory remedies for late payments of commercial debts (interest) and calculations
	• Remedies available for collection of outstanding amounts.
1.3	Explain the terms and conditions associated with customer contracts
	• Void, voidable and unenforceable contracts
	• Retention of title clauses
	• Invitation to treat.
1.4	Discuss the data protection and ethical considerations associated with credit control activities
	• The effect of data protection on the organisation and customers
	• Professional ethics in the context of credit control
	• Data protection legislation and the application of the guiding principles
4.2	Discuss the effects of bankruptcy and insolvency
	• Types of personal and company insolvencies and relevant actions
	• Features of liquidation, receivership, administration and bankruptcy
	• Impacts on the organisation

3.1	Discuss legal and administrative procedures for debt collection
	• Small claims, fast-track and multitrack procedures • Garnishee orders, warrants of execution and delivery • Attachment of earnings and charging orders
3.2	Evaluate the effectiveness of methods for collection and management of debts
	• Legal actions and use of statute • Legal processes and types insolvency
3.3	Justify appropriate debt recovery methods
	• Evaluate retention of title claims and recommend actions

Assessment context

Credit Management students must be able to explain the main features of contract law and be able to identify appropriate remedies for any breach of contract when things go wrong. Additionally students need to be aware of other relevant legislation, such as consumer rights, along with data protection legislation.

Qualification context

The legal framework that organisations work within was introduced at Level 2 in the Work Effectively in Finance unit and the importance of data protection expanded upon in the Ethics for Accountants unit at Level 3.

Business context

Contract law is an important area within credit management as this legislation helps to prevent misunderstandings between all parties to a transaction and provides remedies if one party does not fulfil its contracted responsibilities. In the context of credit control this means that debts are collected from customers when due.

Chapter overview

- Late Payment of Commercial Debts (Interest) Act
- The Data Protection Act

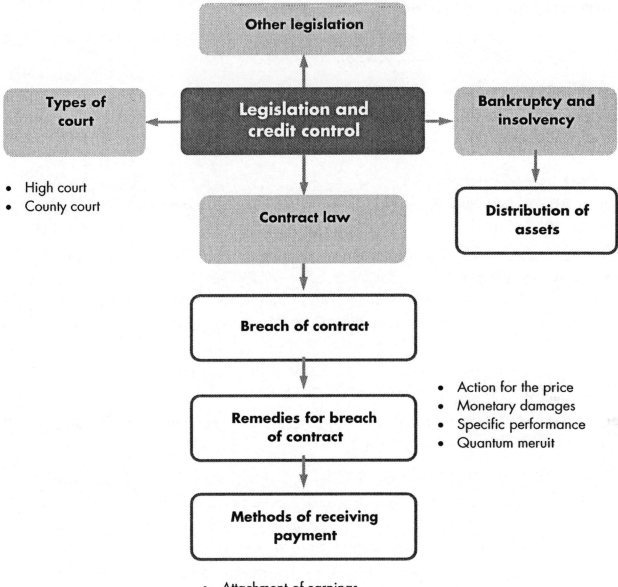

- High court
- County court

- Action for the price
- Monetary damages
- Specific performance
- Quantum meruit

- Attachment of earnings
- Garnishee order
- Receiver
- Charge
- Bankruptcy
- Insolvency
- Warrant of execution

Introduction

Legislation is an important area in credit management as it governs how contracts between parties are enforced.

In this chapter we are going to look at contract law and legal definitions, along with the remedies a party may have if one party does not fulfil its part of a contract.

We will also cover bankruptcy for individuals, sole traders and partnerships, along with liquidation or administration for companies.

Other legislation can be important; these include the Data Protection Act and the Late Payment of Commercial Debts (Interest) Act.

1 Contract law

The relationship between a seller of goods and a buyer of goods is a contract, therefore in this section we must consider the basics of contract law.

What is a contract?

A **contract** may be defined as a legally enforceable agreement between two or more parties.

As an individual you will enter into contracts every day – when you buy goods in a shop, when you place an order for goods over the telephone, when you employ a plumber to fix a leak. These contracts are usually verbal but contracts can also be in writing: for example, if you take out a loan from your bank there will be a written contract.

During your working hours you will also be part of the process of contracts being made between your organisation and its customers and suppliers.

Contracts have three main elements and these are: agreement, consideration (value) and intention to create legal relations.

The importance of contract law

The importance of contract law is that if a contract is validly made between two parties, and if one party does not satisfactorily carry out its side of the agreement, the other party can take the defaulting party to court for **breach of contract**.

How is a contract formed?

For a contract to be formed and to be valid there must be three main elements:

Agreement + Value + Intention to create legal relations = Contract

Agreement

In legal terms, for there to be a valid agreement there must be a valid **offer** and a valid acceptance of that offer.

There will be two parties to a contract – the **offeror** and the **offeree**.

Offeror – is the person making the offer.
Offeree – is the person to whom the offer is made.

Illustration 1

The glass division of SC Fuel and Glass has received a purchase enquiry from a large building contractor concerning the purchase of 1,000 sealed glazed units. For such a large order the glass division is prepared to reduce the price charged from the normal price of £80 to £78 per unit, and has sent out a purchase quotation stating this price for the 1,000 units.

Who is the offerer and offeree?

This will become a valid offer from SC Fuel and Glass to the building contractor when the building contractor receives the purchase quotation in the post. Obviously, it is important that the price quoted is correct as, if not, the building contractor could legally require SC to sell the units to it at the price quoted.

Remember also that an offer can be made verbally, so if quoting a price to a customer over the telephone, ensure that it is the correct price as it will be a valid offer.

The building contractor will become the offeree if it wishes to take up SC Fuel and Glass's offer.

Activity 1: Offerer and offeree

A newsagent is open for business when a customer enters, picks up a magazine and pays the shop owner.

Required

Who is the offeror and offeree in this situation?

An invitation to treat

Care must be taken to distinguish between an offer and an **invitation to treat**. An invitation to treat is an invitation by the seller of goods for the buyer to make an offer to buy them at that price. Examples of invitations to treat are advertisements for goods, catalogues and price tickets displayed on goods.

Illustration 2

The glass division of SC Fuel and Glass issues a catalogue to potential and existing customers twice a year, showing the different types of double-glazed units available and their prices.

Is this an offer or an invitation to treat?

This is an invitation to treat and not an offer, therefore SC is not necessarily tied to the prices quoted in the catalogue. If a customer enquires about purchasing goods from the catalogue then they are making an offer to buy the goods at the catalogue price. It is then up to SC to decide whether or not to accept this offer by selling to the customer at the published price – or changing the price if circumstances have changed.

Activity 2: Invitation to treat or an offer?

It is a rainy afternoon and a goods shop has a stand of umbrellas outside, all priced for sale at £2.99 each.

Required

Is this an example of an invitation to treat or an offer?

Activity 3: Pricing error

Jon is in a car showroom and sees a price ticket on a car of £2,395. He offers to buy the car at this price but is informed by the salesman that there was an error on the price ticket, which should have read £12,395.

Required

Explain whether Jon can insist on purchasing the car at £2,395.

Duration of an offer

If an offer is made then it does not have to remain in place indefinitely. There are a number of ways in which an offer can be brought to an end:

- If there is a set time period for an offer, then the offer will lapse at the end of that time period. If there is no express time period set then the offer will lapse after a reasonable period of time.

- An offer can be revoked by the offeror at any point in time before it has been accepted. **Revocation of an offer** means that the offer is cancelled.

- An offer comes to an end if it is rejected. Care must be taken here, as rejection need not only be by the offeree specifically saying 'no' to the offer. An offer is also rejected by a **counter-offer**. For example, if an offer is made to sell an item for £1,000 and the offeree replies to say that he will buy it at a price of £900 this is a rejection of the original offer to sell.

- The offer also comes to an end when a valid **acceptance** is made.

Acceptance of an offer

The acceptance of an offer must be an absolute and unqualified acceptance.

- Acceptance can be made verbally or in writing.

- If an offer requires a particular form of acceptance (such as verbal, in writing or by fax) then this is the form in which the acceptance must be made.

- The acceptance must be unqualified – if any additional conditions or terms are included in an acceptance then this takes the form of a counter-offer, which rejects the original offer.

Activity 4: Changes to an offer

A homeowner has instructed a builder to construct a brick wall in his garden. A contract has been agreed and a payment made to cover the costs of materials. Part way through the work the homeowner requests that the wall is to be decorated with expensive decorative bricks.

Required

Explain how this affects the contract between the homeowner and builder.

Value

The second required element of a contract is that of there being some value. The basis of contract law is that we are dealing with a bargain of some sort, not just a promise by one of the parties to a contract to do something.

What is required for there to be a valid contract is known in legal terms as **consideration**. Consideration can be thought of as something given, promised or done in exchange for the action of the other party.

In terms of business transactions, the consideration given for a sale of goods is either the money paid now or the promise by a receivable to pay at a later date.

Both parties must bring something of value to the contract for it to be legally binding, ie valid. It can be something of money's worth; for example, you could give your pen for someone's car in return. Both of these have value – but note that consideration does not have to be of equal value, or reflect market value. There is no remedy in law for a bad bargain!

Activity 5: Essentials of a valid contract

A cyclist has a puncture and has taken her bike into a cycling shop for repair. The shop owner has stated that, as he has some spare time, he would be happy to repair the tyre free of charge.

Required

Explain whether there is a valid contract between the cyclist and shop owner.

Diagram of a valid contract

Tomahawk Telecom Ltd (TT Ltd) has a high street shop that sells mobile telephones. TT publishes a regular brochure that gives details of telephones for sale and their prices. TT's brochure is an invitation to treat.

If a customer contacts the shop to purchase a telephone out of the brochure then this is an offer at the price given in the brochure for the telephone. The customer is the offeror.

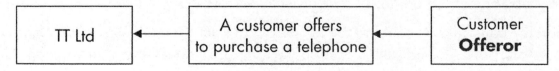

TT Ltd now has the option to accept this offer. TT Ltd is the offeree as it is the party to which the offer is made.

Value has to pass between offeror and offeree so that there is a valid contract. This is called **consideration**. In this example the **consideration** is the mobile telephone and money exchanging between TT Ltd and the customer.

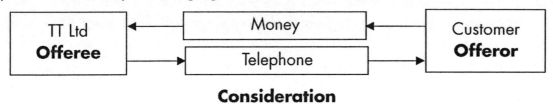

Consideration

Unilateral contracts

Most contracts are known as **bilateral contracts**, meaning that two persons or parties have taken action to form a contract. **Unilateral contracts** involve an action undertaken by one person or group alone. In contract law, unilateral contracts allow only one person to make a promise or agreement, so only they are under an enforceable obligation.

A common example of a unilateral contract is with insurance contracts. The insurance company promises it will pay the insured person a specific amount of money if a certain event happens. If the event doesn't happen, the company won't have to pay. The insured party doesn't make any promise and, to keep his part of the deal, only needs to pay the insurance premium.

Defective contracts

There are some situations in which a contract will only have limited legal effect – or even no legal effect at all.

A **void contract** is not a contract at all. The parties are not bound by it and if they transfer property under it, they can sometimes recover their goods – even from a third party. This normally comes about due to some form of common mistake on a fundamental issue of the contract.

A **voidable contract** is a contract which one party may set aside. Property transferred before avoidance is usually irrecoverable from a third party. Such contracts may be with minors, or contracts induced by misrepresentation, duress or undue influence. In these cases it can be deemed that a party did not have the legal capacity to consent to a contract. Examples here can be intoxication, mental health or being too young to enter into a contract.

An **unenforceable contract** is a valid contract; property transferred under it cannot be recovered, even from the other party to the contract. But if either party refuses to perform or to complete their part of the performance of the contract, the other party cannot compel them to do so. A contract is usually unenforceable when the required evidence of its terms, for example, written evidence of a contract relating to land, is not available.

2 Breach of contract

Parties to a contract can take the other to court for breach of contract. Breach of contract is where one party to the contract does not fulfil his part of the agreement.

Terms in a contract

In most contracts there are certain **terms** that must be fulfilled in order for the contract to be carried out. If the terms of a contract are not fulfilled then one party will be in breach of contract. Legally, different terms of a contract have different effects.

Express terms are terms that are specifically stated in the contract and are binding on both parties.

Conditions are terms that are fundamental to the contract and, if they are broken, then the party breaking them will be in breach of contract and can be sued for damages. The injured party can regard the contract as ended.

Warranties are less important terms in a contract. If any of these are not fulfilled then there is breach of contract but the contract remains in force. The injured party can still claim damages from the court for any loss suffered, but he cannot treat the contract as terminated.

Implied terms are terms of a contract which are not specifically stated but are implied in such a contract, either by trade custom or by the law.

Remedies for breach of contract

A breach of contract arises where one party to the contract does not carry out its side of the bargain, such as a credit customer who does not pay. There are a number of remedies available to the injured party for breach of contract.

These include:

- Action for the price – a court action to recover the agreed price of the goods/services
- Monetary damages – compensation for loss
- Termination – one party refusing to carry on with the contract
- Specific performance – a court order that one of the parties must fulfil its obligations
- Quantum meruit – payment ordered for the part of the contract performed
- Injunction – one party to the contract being ordered by the court not to do something

In terms of a credit customer not having paid for goods or services provided, the most appropriate remedy would normally be an action for the price.

Assessment focus point

In the assessment you may have to suggest an appropriate remedy for a breach of contract. If this is asked for, you should take into account all available information and look for the best outcome to the injured party. Normally, action for the price will give a better outcome for the seller compared to monetary damages, as the full selling price can be recovered.

Activity 6: Remedy for breach of contract

A trader has sold and delivered goods to a credit customer; however, the customer is now refusing to pay for the goods. The goods originally cost the trader £60 and the selling price to the customer was £100.

Required

Identify the most appropriate remedy available to the trader.

Activity 7: Remedy for breach of contract

A gardener has entered into a contract with a land owner to cut six trees. After three trees have been cut, the land owner states he has changed his mind and now wishes to cancel the work.

Required

Identify the most appropriate remedy for the gardener to recover payment.

Restitutionary and compensatory damages

Restitutionary damages aim to strip, from a wrongdoer, any gains made by committing a wrong or breaching a contract. They are concerned with the reversal of benefits that have been earned unjustly by the defendant at the expense of the claimant.

A real-life example of restitutionary damages is the British spy who, as part of his contract of employment, had signed the Official Secrets Act. The spy later breached his contract by divulging state secrets in his memoirs. The British Government duly sued the spy for the profits made on his book.

If the monetary remedy or damages is to be the loss made by the claimant, these are known as **compensatory damages**, and are intended to provide the claimant with the monetary amount necessary to replace what was lost and nothing more. Common examples of compensatory damages are lost wages or income.

Bringing a dispute to court

If it is decided that the only course of action to recover money owed by a credit customer is that of legal action, then the first step is to instruct a solicitor. The solicitor will require details of the goods or services provided, the date the liability arose, the exact name and trading status of the customer, any background information (such as disputes in the past) and a copy of any invoices that are unpaid.

Assessment focus point

When considering court action bear in mind that it may not be viable to bring a customer to court for outstanding debts. The use of a solicitor can be expensive and the court process time-consuming. If the debt is a small amount and/or if there is some doubt the customer can pay then it may, in some circumstances, be appropriate to write the amount off as irrecoverable.

Which court?

Outstanding amounts owed to an entity are civil claims. Uncomplicated claims with a value under £10,000 will be dealt with in the County Court under the **Small Claims Track** (sometimes known to the lay public as 'Small Claims Court' although it is not a separate court). Claims between £10,000 and £25,000 that are capable of being tried within one day are allocated to the 'fast track'; claims over £25,000, or very complex cases where the amount is less than £25,000 but will require more than one day in court, are allocated to the 'multi-track' route. Most cases will be heard in the County Court, but very complex or high-value cases will be heard by the High Court. A judge will decide if the case will be dealt with in a 'fast track' or 'multi-track' hearing once initial paperwork has been filed by the claimant and the defendant. For more information on procedures please see forms EX305 and EX306 produced by Her Majesty's Courts and Tribunal Services.

Hierarchy of civil courts
High Court For complex cases Claims over £25,000
County Court Claims between £10,000 to £25,000
County Court Small claims division Claims less than £10,000

Activity 8: Type of court

An action is to be brought against a customer for unpaid amounts of £5,000.

Required

In which court would this action normally be brought?

	✓
County Court	
Magistrates' Court	
High Court	
Employment Tribunal	

Methods of receiving payment under a court order

Once there has been a court order that the money due must be paid, there are a number of methods of achieving this:

Attachment of earnings order	The business will be paid the amount owing directly by the customer's employer, as a certain amount is deducted from their weekly/monthly pay. However this is only viable for a customer who is an individual and is in stable, consistent work.
Third-party debt order (garnishee order)	This allows the business to be paid directly by a third party who owes the business's customer money.

Warrant of execution	A court bailiff seizes and sells the customer's goods on behalf of the business.
Administrative order	The customer makes regular, agreed payments into court to pay off the debt.
Receiver	A receiver is appointed to receive money that will be owing to the customer, eg rents.
Charge	A legal charge is taken on property or financial assets, so the supplier is paid when the assets are sold.
Bankruptcy	See next section.
Liquidation	See next section.

Illustration 3

SC Fuel and Glass is owed £2,800 by one of its hauliers, Terence Frame & Sons. The claim was taken to the Small Claims Court and SC Fuel and Glass was successful in its claim against Terence Frame & Sons. During the case it becomes apparent that a third party, Cranford Garages Ltd, owed Terence Frame & Sons £4,000. To this date Terence Frame & Sons has had a very poor record in paying its suppliers.

What arrangement would be most suitable here for SC Fuel and Glass to receive payment?

Conclusion: The most appropriate arrangement here would be for the court to order the third party, Cranford Garages Ltd, to pay £2,800 direct to SC Fuel and Glass and then for Cranford Garages Ltd to pay the balance of £1,200 to Terence Frame & Sons. This type of third-party debt order is sometimes referred to as a garnishee order.

Activity 9: Method to receive payment

A customer owes a business £2,000. The customer does not have an income but does own two top of the range laptops. The business intends to take legal action against the customer.

Required

Identify the most appropriate method of payment that the court could award the business.

Assessment focus point

If you are required to suggest a method to receive payment always take into account any information supplied. Is the customer in employment to make payments from – or does he or she have any assets of value that could be sold?

3 Bankruptcy and insolvency

Bankruptcy arises where an individual cannot pay his or her debts and is declared bankrupt.

Insolvency is where a company cannot pay its debts as they fall due.

Petition for bankruptcy

If a trade receivable owes an amount of at least £5,000 a **statutory demand** can be issued for payment of the amount due within a certain period of time. This may result in the customer offering a settlement. If, however, there is no settlement offer from the customer a petition for bankruptcy will be received from the court.

Once the individual has received the statutory demand they have 21 days, either to pay the debt or reach an agreement to settle the outstanding amount.

There are time limits in making a statutory demand and these are:

- The demand should be made within four months of the debt. If the debt is older than four months a court has to be contacted to explain the reasons behind the delay.

- Normally a statutory demand cannot be made after six years have elapsed.

Consequences of a petition for bankruptcy

The consequences of a petition for bankruptcy against a receivable are:

- If the customer pays money to any other suppliers or disposes of any property then these transactions are void.

- Any other legal proceedings relating to the customer's property or debts are suspended.

- An interim receiver is appointed to protect the estate.

Consequences of a bankruptcy order

The consequences of a bankruptcy order are:

- The official receiver takes control of assets.

- A statement of the assets and liabilities is drawn up – this is known as a **statement of affairs**.

- The receiver summons a meeting of creditors of the individual within 12 weeks of the bankruptcy order.

- The creditors of the individual appoint a trustee in bankruptcy.

- The assets are realised and a distribution is made to the various creditors.

- The creditor who presented the petition does not gain any priority for payment over other creditors.

Order of distribution of assets

The assets of the bankrupt will be distributed in the following order:

- Secured creditors

- Bankruptcy costs

- Preferential creditors such as employees, pension schemes, HM Revenue & Customs

- Unsecured creditors, such as trade payables

- The bankrupt's spouse

- The bankrupt

As an unsecured trade payable, a business with debts due from a bankrupt should submit a written claim to the trustee detailing how the debt is made up. This may also need to be substantiated with documentary evidence. As the payment of unsecured creditors comes after many other payments, the supplier may receive little or nothing towards the amount owed. Often this is in the form of a 'dividend': for example, if a bankrupt owed £100,000 to creditors, but has only £20,000 left after other payments have been made, then a trade payable will only receive 20 pence for every pound that it is owed.

Activity 10: Bankruptcy an option?

Haven Limited is one of your firm's clients and is currently facing financial difficulties. The managing director of the company has expressed an opinion that the company will eventually go bankrupt.

Required

Explain how you would respond to the managing director's statement.

Insolvency

The process of insolvency for a company that cannot pay its debts as they fall due is similar to that of a bankrupt individual. There are two main options for companies:

- **Liquidation**
- **Administration**

Liquidation

In a liquidation the company is dissolved and the assets are realised, with debts being paid from the proceeds and any excess being returned to the shareholders. This process is carried out by a liquidator on behalf of the shareholders and/or creditors. The liquidator's job is simply to ensure that the creditors are paid and once this is done the company can be wound up. Again, unsecured creditors are a long way down the list of who is paid first, therefore there may be little left in the pot.

Assessment focus point

Keep in mind that the responsibility of the liquidator is to identify any assets of the troubled company and then distribute to the outstanding creditors, so that the company's debts can be paid as fully as possible. Although the liquidator will act professionally and with fairness towards the company, it is not his or her role to save the company.

Administrative receivership

An alternative to a liquidation is that the shareholders, directors or creditors can present a petition to the court for an administration order. The effect of this is that the company continues to operate but an insolvency practitioner (administrator) is put in control of it, with the purpose of trying to save the company from insolvency, as a going concern – or at least achieve a better result than a liquidation.

Administrative receivership is a process whereby a creditor can enforce security against a company's assets in an effort to obtain repayment of the secured debt. It used to be the most popular method of obtaining payment by secured creditors, but legislative reforms have reduced its significance.

Administrative receivership differs from liquidation in that an administrative receiver is appointed over all of the assets and undertakings of the company. This means that an administrative receiver can normally only be appointed by the holder of a floating charge. Usually an administrative receiver will be an accountant with considerable experience of insolvency matters.

Retention of title clause

A **'retention of title' clause** can be written into agreements with customers. Such a clause states that the buyer does not obtain ownership of the goods unless and until payment is made. Accordingly, if the buyer does go out of business before paying for the goods, the supplier can retrieve them. If payment is not made goods can be stopped in transit and a lien secured on the goods by the seller.

Assessment focus point

Look out for use of retention of title clauses in the assessment. The key here is who actually own the goods. These types of clauses included into contracts stipulate the ownership of (or title to) the goods remains with the seller until the buyer actually makes payment. Problems can arise, though, when it is difficult to identify the goods delivered, for example coal or if the 'buyer' has since sold the goods on. This is where the courts can be needed in making a final decision.

Activity 11: Bankruptcy and insolvency

Outline the main differences between bankruptcy and insolvency.

4 Other legislation

Trade Descriptions Act

The Trade Descriptions Act makes it a criminal offence to declare false or misleading statements about goods being sold or services being provided.

For example, if a business stated that a particular product was now being sold for £24.99, reduced from £49.99, this would be a criminal offence if, in fact, the product had previously been sold at a price of £39.99.

Consumer Rights Act

The purpose of this legislation is to protect the rights of consumers when entering into contracts for the supply of goods, services and also supplies of digital content. Digital content can include such items as e-book and music downloads.

The Act states that there are three key necessities for the goods. They must be:

- 'Of satisfactory quality' – this is the standard of quality that a reasonable person would expect, given the description of the goods and their price.

- 'Fit for the purpose' – the goods should do what they would be expected to do or what the shop claims they can do.

- 'As described' – the goods must be what they are described to be; for example, an automatic car must have an automatic gearbox.

Where goods are sold on credit, title of ownership passes when goods are ready for delivery. For goods sold by 'sale or return' title passes when the buyer approves the goods (eg does not reject them).

The Act outlines specific rights for consumers. These rights include:

- The right to pre-contract information before a purchase is made.

- Goods supplied have to match any samples shown before a purchase is made.

- A right to a repair or replacement if goods do not match those described.

- If goods supplied do not match those agreed to, the consumer has a 'short-term right to reject' with a time limit of 30 days – with a final right to reject if the goods still do not match those described.

- If a refund is given to the consumer then no deductions are allowed from the amount repaid.

The Act also requires that contract terms and notices need to be fair, to help ensure that any unfair terms or notices are not included in the 'small print'.

A term or notice can be deemed unfair when it causes a significant inequality to the detriment of the consumer.

Terms or notices that are unfair are not binding on the consumer; however, consumers can still agree to such terms if they so wish.

Consumer Credit Act

This Act gives additional rights to individuals (rather than companies) who are credit customers of a business. The aim of the Act is to ensure that individuals who become credit customers of a business are fully aware of what they have agreed to.

Late Payment of Commercial Debts (Interest) Act

This legislation gives businesses and public sector bodies the right to claim interest from business customers or public sector customers which pay late. It is for the supplier to decide whether or not to make a claim for interest.

The statutory interest rate chargeable is the Bank of England base rate plus 8%. This was set so that businesses could cover late payments by bank borrowings. Interest runs from the day after the credit period if the customer has not paid within the agreed credit period. If there is no agreed credit period, the legislation sets a default credit period of 30 days, after which interest can run. The interest can be calculated using the following formula:

Formula to learn

Gross debt × (Bank of England base rate + 8%) × (number of days late/365)

Once statutory interest runs on a qualifying debt, the supplier is also entitled under the legislation to claim a fixed sum for compensation as follows:

- For debts less than £1,000, the supplier can claim £40.
- For debts between £1,000 and £9,999.99, the supplier can claim £70.
- For debts of £10,000 or more, the supplier can claim £100.

Illustration 4

SC Fuel and Glass is owed an amount of £10,000 plus VAT at 20%. The Bank of England rate is 2% and the debt is 60 days late.

The amount of interest due is £10,000 × 1.2 × 0.10 × 60/365 = 197.26.

Activity 12: Late payment interest

Ajax Alloys Ltd is owed £12,000 plus VAT at 20% from Gable Garage Ltd. The Bank of England rate is 1% and the debt is 40 days late.

Required

Calculate the interest Ajax Alloys Ltd can claim from Gable Garage Ltd under the Late Payment of Commercial Debts (Interest) Act.

5 Data protection

Due to the growth in the use of computer technology the **Data Protection Act** was introduced to restrict the use of data held about individuals and the use of personal data.

The principles of the Act apply to organisations which are collecting or holding information about individuals. As it is likely that organisations which have a credit control department will be processing information on individuals, ie their customers, it is important that the requirements of the Act are complied with for these organisations. One of the requirements of the Act is that every organisation that processes personal information must notify the Information Commissioner's Office (ICO). Notification is effective for one year.

It is important to realise that the Act only relates to personal information data held about individuals and not about organisations, so will only be relevant to non-corporate customers or to data about individuals who belong to a customer organisation.

Within each organisation there has to be a person who has the responsibility of informing the ICO of ongoing information processing or changes. This is the role of the data controller. Once the organisation is registered with the ICO, individual employees do not need to register as they will be covered by their organisation's registration. Of course, if the organisation consists of a sole trader then that person will need to register on his or her own behalf!

Failure to notify the ICO is a criminal offence. The ICO can issue fines up to £500,000 for serious breaches of the Act, so it is essential that organisations are aware of their responsibilities and stay within the law. The ICO continually monitors organisations for any non-compliance of the Act and, as you can see, the penalties can be severe – along with the negative publicity that can surround an enforcement case.

Definitions from the Act

Personal information, held about a living individual, includes not only factual information but also expressions of opinion about that individual.

A **data subject** is an individual who is the subject of personal data.

A **data controller** is a person who holds and processes personal information.

(Data Protection Act, 1998)

Eight principles of good practice

Information should be:

- Fairly and lawfully processed (see below)
- Processed for limited purposes
- Adequate, relevant and not excessive
- Accurate and up to date
- Not kept for longer than necessary
- Processed in line with the data subject's rights
- Kept securely
- Not transferred to countries outside the EU unless such data is adequately protected in those countries

Data subject's rights under the Act

Data subjects have seven rights under the Data Protection Act.

- **The right to subject access** – this allows people to find out what information is held about them on computer and within some manual records.

- **The right to prevent processing** – anyone can ask a data controller not to process data relating to them that causes substantial unwarranted damage or distress to them or anyone else.

- **The right to prevent processing for direct marketing** – anyone can ask a data controller not to process data relating to them for direct marketing purposes.

- **Rights in relation to automated decision taking** – individuals have a right to object to decisions made only by automatic means, eg when there is no human involvement.

- **The right to compensation** – an individual can claim compensation from a data controller for damage and distress caused by any breach of the Act.

- **The right to rectification, blocking, erasure and destruction** – individuals can apply to the courts to order a data controller to rectify, block or destroy personal details if they are inaccurate or contain expression of opinion based on inaccurate data.

- **The right to ask the Commissioner to assess whether the Act has been contravened** – if someone believes their personal information has not been processed in accordance with the Data Protection Act, they can ask the Commissioner to make an assessment. If the Act is found to have been breached then an enforcement notice may be served on the data controller in question.

For further information on the Data Protection Act please visit ico.org.uk.

Activity 13: Customer information

You are a member of a credit control team where the customers are members of the public. A colleague has stated that, as customer information is held in a paper format, it is acceptable to hold excessive and sometimes non-relevant information on customers.

Required

Explain how you should respond to your colleague.

Professional ethics and credit control

The Data Protection Act outlines the legal responsibilities when holding data on individuals, but there is an ethical responsibility to look after data and information properly. The fundamental ethical principle most applicable here is confidentiality, whereby users of information should keep information private and confidential. This is of particular importance when a business holds sensitive information on its customers. For example, this can include names, addresses and bank details.

There can be some instances where confidentiality can be breached and disclosure made. These are:

- When the customer provides permission to release information
- Where there is a legal requirement to disclose
- Where the disclosure is in the public interest

If customer information is not looked after as expected then this can be seen as a breach of the fundamental ethical principle of professional behaviour and can damage the reputation of the business.

Chapter summary

- A contract is a legally binding agreement, enforceable in a court of law.

- For a valid contract to exist there must be agreement, value and an intention to create legal relations.

- For an agreement to exist there must be a valid offer and acceptance.

- An invitation to treat is an invitation to make an offer – advertisements, catalogues and price labels in shops are examples.

- An offer may lapse, be revoked, be rejected, be rejected by a counter-offer or accepted.

- Acceptance may be verbal or in writing.

- The acceptance must be unqualified – if a qualification or an additional term is introduced then this is deemed to be a counter-offer and the original offer is, therefore, rejected.

- A valid agreement must also be supported by consideration – the consideration must be sufficient but it need not be adequate.

- For an agreement to be enforceable in law there must have been an intention to create legal relations when the contract was made.

- If any terms of a contract are not fulfilled then the injured party can sue for damages for breach of contract.

- An agreement between a seller and a buyer of goods/services will normally be a contract and, therefore, if the buyer does not pay for the goods/services they will be in breach of contract; they can then be taken to an appropriate court for remedy – usually an action for the price.

- If the court agrees that the customer must pay the amount due, this can be done by an attachment of earnings order, a garnishee order, a warrant of execution or, in extreme cases, a bankruptcy notice or liquidation.

- If an individual customer is declared bankrupt, or a corporate customer goes into liquidation or administration, the unsecured creditors (such as trade payables) are unlikely to receive all of the amounts due, but may receive some of the outstanding amount.

- The other legislation relevant to credit management are the Consumer Rights Act, the Late Payment of Commercial Debts (Interest) Act and the Consumer Credit Act.

- The Data Protection Act was introduced to ensure that there were certain restrictions about the use of data regarding individuals.

Keywords

- **Acceptance:** The offeree accepts the offer

- **Administration:** A court-appointed administrator takes over the running of the company to try and return the company to solvency

- **Bankruptcy:** An individual cannot pay his or her debts

- **Bilateral contracts:** Contracts undertaken by two persons or parties

- **Breach of contract:** If one party does not carry out the terms of the contract then that party is in breach of contract

- **Compensatory damages:** Damages that are intended to provide the claimant with the monetary amount necessary to replace what was lost, and nothing more

- **Conditions:** Terms that are fundamental to the contract

- **Consideration:** Something given, promised or done in exchange for the action of the other party

- **Contract:** A legally binding agreement, enforceable in a court of law

- **Counter-offer:** If an acceptance is made by an offeree which contains a new term or condition then this is deemed to be a counter-offer, which is a rejection of the original offer. It constitutes a new offer which, in turn, must be accepted by the original offeror for a contract to be made

- **Data controller:** A person who determines the manner in which any personal data is to be processed

- **Data Protection Act:** Law designed to make certain restrictions about the use of data about individuals and the use of personal data

- **Data subject:** An individual who is the subject of personal data

- **Express terms:** Terms that are specifically stated in the contract

- **Implied terms:** Terms of a contract that are not specifically stated but are implied by trade custom or law

- **Insolvency:** A company cannot pay its debts

- **Invitation to treat:** An invitation to another party to make an offer

- **Liquidation:** Termination of a business operation by using its assets to discharge its liabilities

- **Offer:** An expression of willingness to contract on a specific set of terms, which may be verbal or in writing

- **Offeree:** The person to whom the offer has been made

- **Offeror:** The person making an offer in the hope of an acceptance

- **Personal information:** Information held about an individual

- **Restitutionary damages:** Damages that aim to strip from a wrongdoer any gains made by committing a wrong or breaching a contract

- **Retention of title clause:** States that the buyer does not obtain ownership of the goods unless and until payment is made

- **Revocation of an offer:** An offer is revoked if the offeror removes the offer before it is accepted

- **Small claims track:** A court process for uncomplicated lower-value claims

- **Statement of affairs:** A statement of the bankrupt's assets and liabilities

- **Statutory demand:** Final demand for payment which must be issued before a petition for bankruptcy can be made

- **Terms:** Items in the contract that must be carried out to avoid breach of contract occurring

- **Unenforceable contract:** A valid contract but, if either party refuses to perform or to complete their part of the performance of the contract, the other party cannot compel them to do so

- **Unilateral contracts:** Contracts undertaken by one person or group alone

- **Voidable contract:** A contract which one party may set aside

- **Void contract:** Not a contract at all and the parties are not bound by it

- **Warranties:** Less important terms in the contract

Activity answers

Activity 1: Offerer and offeree

The customer is the offeror here, as he or she is offering to purchase the magazine. The newsagent is the offeree, as they are the person to whom the offer is being made.

Activity 2: Invitation to treat or an offer?

This is merely an invitation to treat, as the priced-up umbrellas are there to encourage someone to make an offer to purchase. If a potential customer was to pick up an umbrella, enter the shop and indicate that they wish to purchase an umbrella then this would then be an 'offer'.

Activity 3: Pricing error

Jon cannot insist on purchasing the car at the lower price, as the price ticket is an invitation to treat rather than an offer. Jon makes the offer to buy the car for £2,395 but this is rejected by the salesman.

Activity 4: Changes to an offer

This would be a counter-offer and would be considered a new offer and a new contract. The builder would not be expected to complete the additional work without the new contract terms being accepted.

Activity 5: Essentials of a valid contract

A valid contract would not exist here as the element of value or consideration is missing. If the work is carried out free of charge then consideration would not have passed from the cyclist to the shop owner. This is important: if the puncture was not prepared properly and the cyclist missed an important appointment, then the cyclist would have difficulty in claiming for any loss caused by poor workmanship.

Activity 6: Remedy for breach of contract

The most appropriate remedy here would be 'action for the price' as this would enable the full sales price of £100 to be recovered from the customer. An alternative here could be monetary damages; however, this would only be able to recover compensation for any loss. In these circumstances this would be the £60 the trader had previously paid for the goods.

Activity 7: Remedy for breach of contract

As the cut trees cannot be restored or replaced, then possibly the fairest remedy to both parties would be quantum meruit. Here the customer would pay the gardener

BPP
LEARNING MEDIA

for the work completed. As three out of six trees have been cut then possibly 50% of the original invoice may be agreed upon between both parties.

Activity 8: Type of court

	✓
County Court	✓
Magistrates' Court	
High Court	
Employment Tribunal	

As this amount is below £10,000 the claim will be heard in the County Court under the Small Claims Track.

Activity 9: Method to receive payment

As the customer does not have an income and there is no other information on other interested parties or assets, the most appropriate method of payment would be a warrant of execution. This is where a bailiff seizes and sells a customer's effects – in this case the two laptops.

Activity 10: Bankruptcy an option?

Although the company may be experiencing serious financial difficulties, technically the company itself would not be able to become bankrupt. Bankruptcy is only available for individuals. The appropriate response would be to explain to the managing director that if the company was unable to pay its debts it would become insolvent.

Activity 11: Bankruptcy and insolvency

Bankruptcy	Insolvency
Where an individual is unable to pay debts A receiver appointed to take control of assets Statement of affairs drawn up Assets sold to pay debts	Process for companies that are unable to pay their debts Two options available: liquidation and administration Liquidation – a liquidator appointed to dissolve company and sell assets Administration – an administrator appointed to control company with a view to saving or selling the company as a going concern

Activity 12: Late payment interest

The Late Payment of Commercial Debts (Interest) Act allows interest to be charged on gross amounts for the time outstanding. The rate of interest is the Bank of England rate plus 8%.

£12,000 plus VAT £2,400 (£12,000 × 20%) = £14,400.

£14,400 × 9% (1% + 8%) = £1,296

£1,296 × (40/365 days) = £142.03

Activity 13: Customer information

Your colleague is incorrect and you would need to explain that the Data Protection Act prevents holding excess and non-relevant information on both hard-copy and soft-copy media.

1 **What are the three main elements that must exist for a contract to be valid?**

    A   Offer, acceptance and value

    B   Offer, acceptance and valid terms

    C   Agreement, acceptance and value

    D   Agreement, value and intention to create legal relations

2 Alan sees an advertisement in the local newspaper for a car costing £3,000. He answers the advert, saying that he would like to buy the car. He is told by the seller that there was a printing error and the advertisement should have read £5,000.

Can Alan insist on buying the car at £3,000? Explain the reason for your answer.

3 A business sends out a purchase quotation to a customer for goods at a cost of £15,000. The customer replies that he would like to accept the quotation but requires that the goods are delivered the next day.

Does the business have to provide the goods at this price of £15,000?

Explain the reasons for your answer.

4 **What is a condition in a contract?**

    A   A fundamental term of a contract

    B   A term expressly stated in the contract

    C   A term not expressly stated in the contract

    D   A term in the contract which is of lesser importance

5 One of the legal remedies available for a breach of contract is 'Quantum meruit'.

What type of remedy is this?

    A   Compensation for loss

    B   Payment for part of the contract performed

    C   Recovery of agreed price

    D   Refusal to carry on with the contract

6 **What is a garnishee order?**

    A   Amount owing paid by customer's employer

    B   Seizure of assets

    C   Payment by a third party

    D   Regular payments to the court

7 **Explain the purpose of including a 'retention of title' clause within a contract.**

8 **What are the eight principles of good practice of the Data Protection Act regarding the handling of personal information?**

9 **What are the seven data subject's rights under the Data Protection Act?**

Methods of credit control

4

Learning outcomes

3.1	Discuss the legal and administrative procedure for debt collection
	• Role of debt collection agencies and solicitors
3.2	Evaluate the effectiveness of methods for collection and management of debts
	• Use of third parties
3.3	Justify appropriate debt recovery methods
	• Select, analyse and recommend appropriate recovery methods
3.4	Calculate the effect of early settlement discounts and advise management on their use
	• Quantify the effect of discounts on liquidity and cash flow
	• Calculate the annual equivalent cost of using simple or compound interest
	• Present recommendations
4.1	Explain the importance of liquidity management
	• The impact of liquidity of discounts and changes to credit terms
	• Invoice discounting, factoring and credit insurance
	• Calculations relating to factoring, invoice discounting and credit insurance
5.1	Select relevant, accurate and timely information and present it effectively
	• Liaise with debt collection agencies and solicitors
	• Make recommendations with supporting calculations and assess the impact on liquidity

Assessment context

Students should be able to calculate settlement discounts and be able to explain a range of methods that can be used to assist in both credit management and control. This can include the use of third parties such as invoice discounting, factoring services and debt or credit insurance.

Qualification context

Students of Credit Management will meet a new formula in this chapter of the Course Book. This is the settlement discount formula and it is used to quantify the effects of discounts.

Business context

To maintain a healthy cash flow, businesses will need to reduce any risk of incurring irrecoverable debts along with encouraging customers to settle their accounts as early as possible. Methods that can be used here are offering discounts and use of third-party services that can help in recovering payment. There are costs involved in using such credit control methods and individual businesses will need to weigh the costs and benefits before deciding on a credit control strategy for their individual circumstances.

Chapter overview

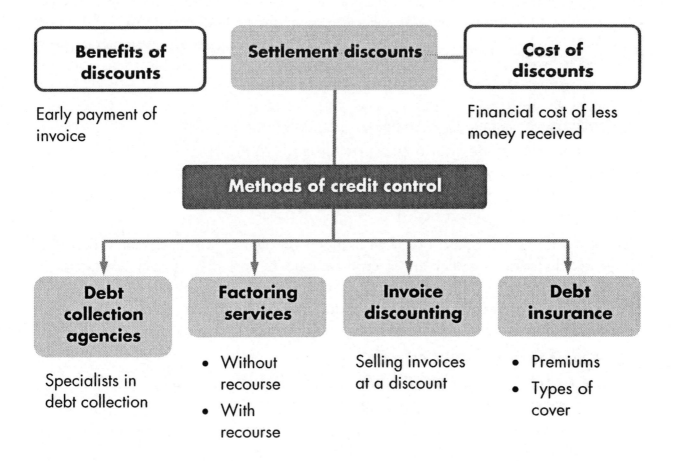

Introduction

Settlement or cash discounts can be offered to customers to encourage early payment. However, this can be expensive due to the loss of income.

Third-party services can also be used to assist in credit management and control. These can include the use of debt collection agencies and finance houses which can provide credit on the basis of amounts owed to the business by customers. These can also be expensive, in addition to the possible loss of goodwill from customers when using such services.

1 Settlement discounts

When offering to trade with a customer on credit terms, a credit limit must be set and the terms of payment communicated to the customer. These terms, such as net 30 days, must be clearly stated to the customer in writing and be on all invoices, statements etc sent to the customer.

One of the terms of trading on credit that can be offered to a customer is that of a settlement discount. A settlement or cash discount is an incentive to the customer to pay its outstanding invoices earlier. A percentage discount off the invoice total is offered if the customer pays within a certain period, which would be shorter than the stated, normal credit terms.

Benefits of a settlement discount

The benefit to a business of offering a settlement discount to credit customers is that, if the customers take up the discount, the money will be received earlier. This means that it can be either invested to earn interest or can be used to reduce any overdraft balance, thereby reducing the amount of interest paid.

Costs of a settlement discount

The cost of a settlement discount is the discount deducted from the face value of the invoice. This results in less money being received by the business although, of course, it is received sooner.

Formula to learn

It is possible to approximate the **annual cost of offering a settlement discount** to customers by using the following formula:

$$\frac{d}{100-d} \times \frac{365}{N-D} \times 100$$

Where   d = Discount percentage given

             N = Normal payment term

             D = Discount payment term

Assessment focus point

You must learn the above formula, as it is unlikely that the formula will be given to you in the assessment. The formula requires repeated practice to commit to memory.

Illustration 1

A business currently trades on 30-day terms but is considering offering a settlement discount of 2% for payment within 14 days of the invoice date.

Calculation of annual cost of settlement discount

Formula to use:

$$\frac{d}{100-d} \times \frac{365}{N-D} \times 100$$

Enter given information into the formula:

$$\frac{2}{100-2} \times \frac{365}{30-14} \times 100$$

Formula becomes:

$$\frac{2}{98} \times \frac{365}{16} \times 100$$

$(0.0204081 \times 22.8125) \times 100$

0.4655597×100

Annual cost of settlement discount = 46.56% (rounded to two decimal places)

As it would cost in excess of 46% per annum to offer this discount it would probably be cheaper to borrow from the bank to raise funds required, at a rate of say 5% or 6%.

Activity 1: Settlement discount cost

A business currently trades on 30-day credit terms but is considering offering a settlement discount of 1% for payment within 10 days of the invoice date.

Required

Identify the annual percentage cost of the settlement discount.

	✓
18.4%	
184.3%	
1.8%	
1.0%	

Activity 2: Settlement discount cost

A business currently trades on 60-day credit terms but is considering offering a settlement discount of 2% for payment within 14 days of the invoice date.

Required

Identify the annual percentage cost of the settlement discount.

	✓
2.0%	
1.62%	
16.2%	
162.0%	

Assessment focus point

Considerations when calculating settlement discount percentages:

You may find you have a long number in your calculator when calculating the d/100-d part of the formula. For greater accuracy calculate the 365/N-D part first, so that you can leave the first part of the calculation in your calculator.

Remember to multiply your answer by 100 to reach a final percentage value. This will, of course, make a big difference to the final answer. For example, 50 as a percentage of 200 is 25% and not 0.25.

Use a 'reasonableness test' to see if your final answer looks sensible. If your answer appears very small or large it may be worth double-checking your calculations.

It is more accurate to leave rounding until you have reached your final percentage figure.

Compound interest and settlement discount costs

The previous examples use a simple interest basis and this is the most normal form of the settlement discount type of calculation. However, some businesses may choose to calculate settlement discount costs on a compound interest basis.

The compound interest method of calculation will result in a higher percentage cost as results are compounded over time, when compared to interest calculated on a simple basis. This is because interest is added to the principal when the compound interest method is used.

For example, £1,000 at 10% over 2 years can be calculated as follows:

Simple interest: Year 1 interest £100, Year 2 interest £100.

Compound interest: Year 1 interest £100, Year 2 interest £110 (£1,100 × 10%).

Although the calculations can be more complex, the use of a scientific calculator can quickly calculate the required answer.

Illustration 2

A business currently trades on 30-day credit terms and is considering offering a 1% settlement discount for payment within 14 days of the invoice date.

The business uses the compound interest basis to calculate settlement discount costs and the calculations are:

$$\frac{1}{99} = 0.0101$$

$$\frac{365}{30-14} = 22.8125$$

$$1 + 0.0101 = 1.0101$$

$$1.0101{\wedge}22.8125 = 1.25765$$

$$1.25765 - 1 = 0.25765$$

$$0.25765 \times 100 = 25.765\%$$

(The ^ symbol in the formula represents 'to the power of' and restates values into a compound interest basis. This function can be found on scientific calculators on the x^y key.)

Increasing credit terms

The granting of a cash discount has a positive effect on the cash flow of the business if the discount is taken up by customers.

Increasing credit terms for a customer has the opposite effect. If an increase in credit terms for a customer were agreed, for example, increasing its credit period from 30 days to 45 days, this would decrease the cash flow to the business as money from this customer would be coming into the business later. If sales revenue increases it is likely there will be a corresponding increase in receivables and an increase in receivables along with the associated increase in any finance costs.

Illustration 3

A company is proposing to increase the credit period to customers from one month to two months. Annual revenue is expected to increase from £1.2 million to £1.8 million and the bank interest cost to the company is 5%.

Calculations for increase in finance cost:

1. Current value of receivables £100,000 (£1.2m/12 months)

2. New receivables: £300,000 (£1.8m × 2/12 months)

3. Increase in receivables £200,000 (£300,000 – £100,000)

4. Additional finance cost = £10,000 (£200,000 × 5%) based on the average additional receivables due to increasing the credit period to two months

Activity 3: New receivables and annual finance cost

A business with a turnover of £2.4 million currently trades on 1-month credit terms but is considering offering customers an additional month of credit.

Required

Identify the new value of the trade receivables balance and the annual cost of financing such a policy if the company pays interest on its overdraft at 10% per annum. Select A, B, C or D.

	New receivables £000	Annual finance cost £000	✓
A	200	20	
B	200	40	
C	400	20	
D	400	40	

Presentation of recommendations

When presenting information to management it is important to show any findings or conclusions clearly. When looking at finance costs, such as the settlement discount cost, it is good practice to show the costs and benefits in implementing such a policy. For example, the benefit of the discount will hopefully result in a better liquidity position after taking into account the cost of the discount.

Assessment focus point

Look out for tasks on the assessment that ask for a recommendation. If you are asked for a recommendation then ensure you do provide one – and back-up your conclusion with relevant calculations and focus your answer on the impact on liquidity that any new policy may have.

2 Methods of debt collection

With good credit management and control procedures in place, money will normally be received from credit customers. Sometimes encouragement such as reminder letters or telephone calls will be needed but payment should eventually be received. However, there will be some cases in which either the debt is never collected and has to be written off as an irrecoverable debt or where the business has to resort to legal procedures to obtain payment.

There are specific methods that a business can use to minimise the possibility of either the loss of the debt or resorting to legal procedures. There are a variety of different methods of collecting the debts that are due and there are costs and benefits of each of these. They include:

- Liaising with debt collection agencies and solicitors
- Factoring
- Invoice discounting
- Debt insurance

Debt collection agencies and solicitors

Debt collection agencies or **credit collection agencies** are commercial organisations that specialise in the collection of debts. Most collection agencies are paid by results and charge a percentage of the debts collected for the business, although some require an advance subscription for their services.

The collection agency will use appropriate methods for collecting the debts and these may include:

- Collection by telephone and letter
- Collection by personal visits
- Negotiation of a payment plan with the customer

Collection agencies are an effective method of collecting debts that are proving difficult to obtain in the normal course of trading. As collection agencies tend to be viewed as a normal business service they are unlikely to have an adverse impact on

the relationship between the business and its customer. However, the collection agency does, of course, charge a fee for its services.

Solicitor services can be utilised in the initial stages of the debt collection process by sending a 'solicitor letter' requesting payment. This can be a cost-effective method of collection as many customers will settle on receipt to avoid further legal action. If the customer still refuses to pay, solicitors will have the knowledge and experience to start the formal legal remedies that are available.

Factoring services

Factoring is a financing service provided by specialist financial institutions, often subsidiaries of major banks, whereby money can be advanced to a company on the basis of the security of their trade receivables. A factor normally provides three main services and a company can take advantage of some or all of these:

- Provision of finance
- Administration of the receivables ledger
- Insurance against irrecoverable debts

Provision of finance by a factor

When sales on credit are made by a business, there will be a period of time elapsing before the money for those sales is received from the business's credit customers. Many businesses may find that they require the cash sooner than the customers are prepared to pay, for example to pay suppliers or reduce an overdraft. This is particularly the case for fast-growing companies.

The factor advances a certain percentage of the book value of the trade receivables, often about 80%, as an immediate payment. The trade receivables are then collected by the factor and the remaining 20%, less a fee, handed over to the business when the amounts are received by the factor.

There is obviously a charge for this service and this will tend to be in two parts:

- A service charge or commission charge
- An interest charge on amounts outstanding

One further hidden cost of factoring can be a loss of customer confidence or goodwill, as customers will be aware that the business has factored its trade receivables; this may have a negative impact on future relations. Many customers will view the use of a factor as an indication that a business is in financial difficulty, despite the increasing use of factoring within business.

Illustration 4

SC Fuel and Glass are considering the use of factor finance in order to pay its own suppliers earlier to take advantage of settlement discounts offered. The book value of the fuel division's trade receivables is currently £700,000. The factor has agreed to advance 80% of this amount and charges 2.5% interest on amounts advanced. The amount advanced is expected to be settled in 30 days. In addition to interest, the factor charges a fixed £1,000 administration fee.

Here SC Fuel and Glass receives £560,000 (80% × £700,000) immediately from the factor.

The factor will then collect the trade receivables on behalf of SC and will pay over the remaining £140,000, less interest charges and administration fee, when settlement has been made by SC's customers.

Interest charges will amount to £1,151 (£560,000 × 2.5% × 30/365) and the £1,000 fixed administration fee will increase total costs for SC Fuel and Glass to £2,151, leaving £137,849 to be settled to SC Fuel and Glass by the factor.

Activity 4: Factoring cost

Hercules Haulage is experiencing liquidity problems and wishes to quickly access cash tied up in trade receivables. Currently, trade receivables stand at £100,000 and a factor will advance 85% of this balance immediately. The factor charges a one-off 2% commission fee on the total receivables balance and charges 5% interest on amounts advanced. It is expected that trade receivables will settle their accounts in 60 days.

Required

Calculate the following amounts.

	£
Amount advanced by the factor	
Factor's commission fee	
Interest payable if receivables pay in 60 days	

Administration of the receivables ledger by a factor

Many factoring arrangements go further than simply providing finance on the security of the trade receivables; they will take over the entire administration of the receivables ledger. This will tend to include the following:

- Assessment of credit status
- Sending out sales invoices
- Recording sales invoices and receipts
- Sending out statements
- Sending out reminders
- Collecting payments from credit customers

The benefit to the business is not only a cost-saving from not having to run its own receivables ledger but also the expertise of the factor in this area. A fee will, of course, be charged for this service – normally based upon a percentage of revenue.

Insurance against irrecoverable debts

If a factor has total control over all aspects of credit management of the receivables ledger then they may be prepared to offer a **without recourse factoring** arrangement.

This means that the factor has no right to claim against the business if a customer does not pay. Effectively, the factor is bearing the risk of any irrecoverable debts and, naturally, will charge a higher fee for accepting this additional risk.

In other circumstances the business will retain the risk of irrecoverable debts and this is known as **with recourse factoring**.

Advantages and disadvantages of factoring

The benefits and costs of factoring can be summarised:

Advantages	Disadvantages
Advance of cash which may not be available from other sources	Cost – commission and interest
Specialist debt administration skills of the factor	Potential loss of customer goodwill
Specialist debt collection skills of the factor	Higher costs for credit insurance
Saving on in-house receivables ledger costs	Problems of reverting to in-house debt collection in future
Reduction in irrecoverable debt cost	
Frees up management time	

Activity 5: Services provided by a factor

Factors offer a range of services to their clients.

Required

Identify which one of the following would not be a service provided by a factor.

	✓
Insurance against irrecoverable debts	
Administration of the receivables ledger	
Provision of finance	
Seizure of goods from customers who do not pay	

Activity 6: A disadvantage of using a factor

There can be a number of disadvantages in using a factor.

Required

Identify which one of the following would be considered a disadvantage of using a factor.

	✓
Cost savings	
Reaction of some customers	
Advance of cash	
Reduction in irrecoverable debts	

Invoice discounting

One of the costs of factoring is the potential loss of customer goodwill if it is known that the business is using a factor to collect its debts. The reason for this is that some customers may infer cash flow problems from the use of a factor, which may not give them confidence to continue trading with the business.

An alternative, therefore, is **invoice discounting** which is a service related to factoring. Invoice discounting is where the debts of a business are purchased by the provider of the service at a discount to their face value. The discounter simply provides cash up front to the business at the discounted amount, rather than have any involvement in the business's receivables ledger. Under a confidential invoice discounting agreement the business is still responsible for collecting its own debts and the business's customers will only be aware of the arrangement if they do not pay their debt. As a result, invoice discounting is often chosen by businesses who wish to retain control of their own receivables ledger.

The cost to the business is the discount at which the trade receivables are purchased. Invoice discounting can be used for a portion of the trade receivables only and is therefore often used for a short-term or one-off exceptional cash requirement.

> ## Assessment focus point
>
> Although the names are similar be sure not to confuse settlement discounts and invoice discounting. These are two different methods of credit management. As a reminder a settlement discount is where a customer takes advantage of a reduction in an invoice value for early payment; invoice discounting is where invoices are sold to a third party for less than their face value.

Activity 7: Invoice discounting and factoring

Two methods of credit management and control are the use of invoice discounting and factoring.

Required

Distinguish between invoice discounting and factoring arrangements.

Debt insurance

Debt insurance is insurance cover taken out against the incurring of irrecoverable debts. It has nothing to do with advances of money or collection of trade receivables (as with factoring) but is simply an insurance policy to cover debts which become irrecoverable and are never settled by the customer.

Such insurance, also known as credit insurance, is available from a number of sources and there are several types of policy available.

Types of insurance policy

The most common policy is a **whole turnover policy**. This type of policy can operate in one of two ways:

- The entire receivables ledger can be covered, but the amount paid out for any irrecoverable debt claim would only be normally about 80% of the claim.

- Alternatively, approximately 80% of the trade receivables can be insured for their entire amount and any claim on these trade receivables would be paid in full.

Either way under this type of policy only a proportion of irrecoverable debts will be covered for loss.

A further type of policy is an **annual aggregate excess policy** where irrecoverable debts are insured in total above an agreed limit or excess, in a similar way to household or car insurance policies.

It is possible to purchase insurance for a specific receivable account rather than receivables in total.

The cost of insurance will differ depending upon the insurer and the type of policy, but premiums tend to be 1–2% of the amounts insured.

Illustration 5

SC Fuel and Glass had a whole turnover policy covering 80% of irrecoverable debts. A customer has been declared bankrupt, owing SC Fuel £120,000 including VAT.

Assuming the VAT element of £20,000 (120,000/1.2 × 0.2) can be claimed back from HMRC, the remaining net amount of £100,000 will then be claimed under the insurance policy. SC Fuel will receive 80% (£80,000) from the insurance company and the balance of £20,000 will be written off as an irrecoverable debt.

Activity 8: Debt insurance claim

A company pays a premium for a whole turnover debt insurance covering 75% of any irrecoverable debts. One customer owes £19,800 including VAT at 20% and the company intends to claim the VAT back from HMRC. The company will claim the maximum allowed under their debt insurance policy.

Required

Calculate how much the company can claim under debt insurance.

Activity 9: Type of insurance policy

A business has insured its total irrecoverable debts above an agreed limit of £2,500.

Required

Identify the type of insurance policy this is.

	✓
Partial turnover policy	
Whole turnover policy	
Specific receivables' policy	
Annual aggregate excess policy	

Chapter summary

- In agreeing credit terms with a customer it may be that the customer is offered a settlement discount for payment earlier than the agreed credit period – although this has a benefit to the seller in that the cash is received sooner, it also has a cost in that less is received due to the discount.

- If amounts due from credit customers cannot be recovered in the normal course of business there are a variety of other alternatives.

- A debt collection agency will use appropriate methods for collecting trade receivables on a business's behalf without normally affecting customer goodwill – a fee will be charged for the agency's services.

- A factoring agreement can be for the provision of finance, the administration of the receivables ledger and may include a 'without recourse' agreement for protection against irrecoverable debts.

- The fees charged by a factor will depend upon the level of service provided, but it can also affect customer goodwill

- Benefits of factoring include an advance of cash, specialist services of the factor and a reduction in the receivables ledger and management time and costs.

- Invoice discounting is similar to factoring although, as it is anonymous, it will not tend to affect customer goodwill and can be used for a portion of trade receivables.

- Debt insurance is not a method of collecting trade receivables but of insuring against the risk of irrecoverable debts.

Keywords

- **Annual aggregate excess policy:** Irrecoverable debts are insured for an amount above an agreed limit or excess

- **Annual cost of offering settlement discount (simple interest method):**
$$\frac{d}{100-d}\times\frac{365}{N-D}\times100\%$$

- **Debt and credit collection agencies:** Commercial organisations that specialise in the collection of trade receivables

- **Debt insurance:** Insurance cover for irrecoverable debts, either for the majority of the receivables ledger or for specific receivables ledger accounts

- **Factoring:** A service whereby a factor advances money on the security of a business's trade receivables and may also provide other services, such as administration of the receivables ledger

- **Invoice discounting:** A service whereby sales invoices are purchased for cash immediately at a discount to their face value

- **Settlement or cash discount:** Discount offered to customers for payment of the due amount earlier than the normal credit terms

- **Whole turnover policy:** Insurance for the whole receivables ledger for, say, 80% of irrecoverable debts; or for 80% of the receivables ledger for all irrecoverable debts

- **With recourse factoring:** A factoring arrangement where the business retains the risk of irrecoverable debts

- **Without recourse factoring:** A factoring arrangement where the factor bears all the risk of irrecoverable debts

Activity answers

Activity 1: Settlement discount cost

	✔
18.4%	✔
184.3%	
1.8%	
1.0%	

$$\frac{1}{99} \times \frac{365}{30-10} = 18.4\%$$

Activity 2: Settlement discount cost

	✔
2.0%	
1.62%	
16.2%	✔
162.0%	

$$\frac{2}{98} \times \frac{365}{60-14} = 16.2\%$$

Activity 3: New receivables and annual finance cost

	New receivables £000	Annual finance cost £000	✔
A	200	20	
B	200	40	
C	400	20	
D	400	40	✔

Current receivables = £2.4m/12 = £200,000

New receivables = £2.4m × 2/12 = £400,000

Annual finance required for the extra £400,000 tied up in working capital at 10% = £40,000.

Activity 4: Factoring cost

	£
Amount advanced by the factor	85,000
Factor's commission fee	2,000
Interest payable if receivables pay in 60 days	699

£100,000 × 85% = £85,000

£100,000 × 2% = £2,000

£85,000 × 5% × 60/365 = £699

Activity 5: Services provided by a factor

	✓
Insurance against irrecoverable debts	
Administration of the receivables ledger	
Provision of finance	
Seizure of goods from customers who do not pay	✓

Activity 6: A disadvantage of using a factor

	✓
Cost savings	
Reaction of some customers	✓
Advance of cash	
Reduction in irrecoverable debts	

Some customers may view the use of a factor by a business as a sign that the business is in financial or cash flow difficulty and therefore may re-consider whether to carry on trading with them.

Activity 7: Invoice discounting and factoring

Invoice discounting is simply the provision of finance to a business by the purchase of its invoices at a discount. There is no involvement with the business's receivables ledger. Under a factoring agreement the factor will normally run the receivables ledger and collect the debts, as well as providing finance in the form of an advance on a percentage of the face value of the receivables.

Activity 8: Debt insurance claim

The amount that can be claimed under debt insurance is £12,375.

The VAT element can be reclaimed from HMRC. £19,800/1.2 × 0.20 = £3,300.

The debt insurance will then be claimed on the net amount of £16,500 (£19,800 – £3,300) × 75% = £12,375.

£4,125 (£16,500 – £12,375) will be written off as an irrecoverable debt.

Activity 9: Type of insurance policy

	✓
Partial turnover policy	
Whole turnover policy	
Specific receivables' policy	
Annual aggregate excess policy	✓

1   Your company currently has an average credit period of 45 days but is considering offering a 2% settlement discount for payment within ten days.

   Using the simple method, what is the approximate annual cost of this discount?

   A   2.0%
   B   2.13%
   C   21.3%
   D   213.0%

2   Factoring arrangements may be either without recourse factoring or with recourse factoring.

   Viewed from the perspective of the company which of the following correctly describes one of these methods?

   A   Without recourse factoring does not cover irrecoverable debts

   B   With recourse factoring does cover irrecoverable debts

   C   Without recourse factoring does cover irrecoverable debts

   D   With recourse factoring does not cover irrecoverable debts

3   **Which of the following is not a cost of using a factoring service for receivables ledger administration and collection of debts?**

   A   Advance of cash
   B   Commission charges
   C   Loss of goodwill
   D   Reverting back to in-house receivables ledger administration

4   **Explain two types of debt insurance policy that a business could take out.**

5   A company has a receivable outstanding amounting to £2,400 including VAT at 20%. The company is able to claim 90% of unpaid debts under their debt insurance policy. Assume the VAT element can be reclaimed from HMRC. **Calculate the amount that can be claimed under the policy and any amount to be written off as irrecoverable.**

Managing the
supply of credit

5

Learning outcomes

3.1	Discuss legal and administrative procedures for debt collection
	• The importance of stages in the debt collection process
3.2	Evaluate the effectiveness of methods for collection and management of debts
	• Organisational policies and procedures • Methods of effective internal and external communication
4.3	Analyse receivables
	• Analyse receivables, trading history and average periods of credit • Apply the 80/20 rule, materiality and status reports • Analyse ledger balances and take corrective action • Calculate and recommend actions on irrecoverable and doubtful debts
4.4	Employ a professional and ethical approach to communications and negotiations with customers
	• Prepare briefing notes for management • Draft letters to customers
5.2	Evaluate recommendations for write-offs and provisions
	• Justify and calculate write-offs and provisions • Analyse the impact on cash flow • Apply professional ethics • Calculate VAT implications

Assessment context

Credit Management students must be able to interpret an aged receivables analysis and apply a credit control policy to identify any issues and decide upon appropriate actions. Students must also be able to identify irrecoverable debts and make allowances for doubtful debts suggesting action points on how they can be dealt with.

Qualification context

The production of aged receivables reports can appear at Level 2 in the Using Accounting Software unit and bookkeeping for irrecoverable and doubtful debt allowances are covered at Level 3 in the Advanced Bookkeeping unit.

Business context

Effective cash management will include the use of a debt collection policy to guide on actions to take when issues are identified from the aged receivables report or from other available credit information. Actions to take can include reminder telephone calls through to more serious processes, such as legal action.

Chapter overview

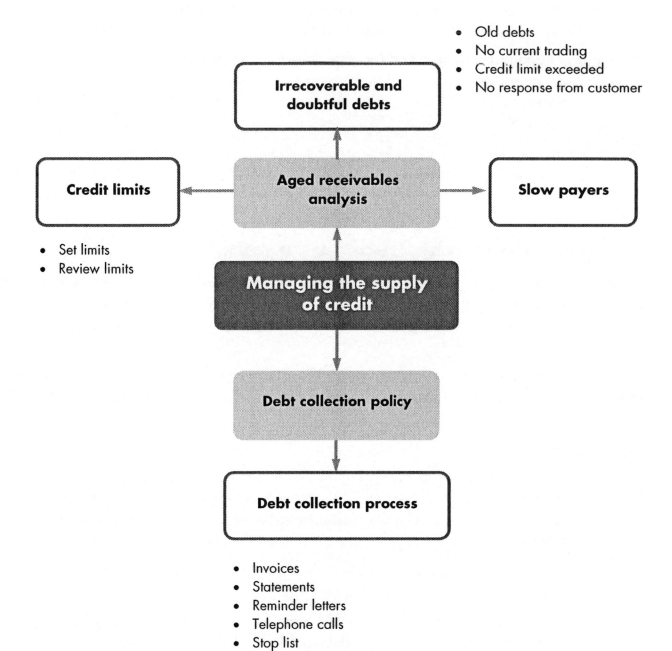

- Old debts
- No current trading
- Credit limit exceeded
- No response from customer

Irrecoverable and doubtful debts

Aged receivables analysis

Credit limits

Slow payers

- Set limits
- Review limits

Managing the supply of credit

Debt collection policy

Debt collection process

- Invoices
- Statements
- Reminder letters
- Telephone calls
- Stop list

Introduction

The supply of credit to customers is managed by the business's debt collection policy along with the use of aged receivables reports.

The debt collection policy will outline the appropriate action that should be taken, if any, to encourage payment and the collection of outstanding debts.

Actions will need to be decided on for each individual customer and that customer's own circumstances. For example, would a reminder telephone call be sufficient or should stronger actions be taken – such as sending legal letters or using debt collection agencies?

The aged receivables report will also help identify potential irrecoverable or doubtful debts. Decisions will need to be taken on whether a particular debt should be written off as irrecoverable or to provide an allowance for the amount outstanding.

1 Transactions with credit customers

Once it has been agreed with a customer that they may trade on credit terms with the business, an account will be set up for that customer in the receivables ledger. The entries in this account will be invoices and credit notes sent to the customer and receipts from the customer.

One of the roles of the credit control team will be to monitor, on a regular basis, the transactions on each receivable's account and, in particular, the balance on the account.

Placing an order

The first step in the monitoring of a credit customer's activities is at the initial stage of each transaction when the customer places an order for more goods. When the initial agreement was made with the customer to trade on credit terms, a **credit limit** will have been set by the credit controller for that customer.

The credit limit is the maximum amount that should be outstanding on the customer's account in the receivables ledger at any point in time.

When a customer places an order, the first step is to check that the value of the order does not take the customer's account over their credit limit. If the value of the order means that the customer's balance exceeds the credit limit then this must be discussed with the customer.

Illustration 1

One of SC Fuel and Glass's customers is Nerrington Engineering. On 14 July 20X8 the balance on its account in the receivables ledger is £4,484.04, which is made up as shown in the table below:

		£
26/04/X8	Invoice 203741	1,350.67
28/05/X8	Invoice 203882	994.60
06/06/X8	Credit note 016452	(103.25)
14/06/X8	Invoice 203903	1,226.57
28/06/X8	Invoice 203911	1,015.45
		4,484.04

On this date Nerrington placed an order for an additional £1,245.60 of fuel.

This will take its account balance over its credit limit of £5,000. The credit controller for the fuel division may decide to make a telephone call to the accountant at Nerrington to explain the situation. From here it may be agreed that Nerrington will arrange payment for £2,242.02 which will pay off invoices 203741 and 203882, less the credit note 016452. Once this has been received it would then be agreed that the new order will be processed and the fuel delivered.

Activity 1: Credit limits

Before trading commences with a credit customer, a credit limit will be agreed between the business and the customer and it is important that this limit should not be exceeded.

Required

Identify the effect if a customer exceeds the agreed credit limit.

	✓
Increasing goodwill with the customer	
Ensuring the cancellation of any settlement discount offered	
Loss of sale	
Increasing the risk of non-payment of the amount due	

Review of customer accounts

As well as checking that each order does not mean that the customer's balance exceeds their credit limit, each customer's account should be monitored on a regular basis. This review should involve looking for debts that are not being paid within the stated credit terms and old debts that have not been paid at all.

In order for this review of customer accounts to be meaningful, it is important that the customer accounts are kept up-to-date and accurate so that the correct balance and position can be seen at any point in time.

2 Aged receivables analysis

One particularly useful method of reviewing customer account balances is by producing an **aged receivables analysis**.

An aged receivables analysis is a method of internal communication that splits the total balance on a customer's account into amounts which have been outstanding for particular periods of time, for example:

- Current – up to 30 days
- 31 to 60 days
- 61 to 90 days
- Over 90 days

Illustration 2

We will return to the account of Nerrington Engineering in the receivables ledger of SC Fuel and Glass. At 30 June 20X8 the account balance is made up as follows:

		£
26/04/X8	Invoice 203741	1,350.67
28/05/X8	Invoice 203882	994.60
06/06/X8	Credit note 016452	(103.25)
14/06/X8	Invoice 203903	1,226.57
28/06/X8	Invoice 203911	1,015.45
		4,484.04

The precise age of each of the outstanding invoices can be shown more clearly if an aged receivables analysis is prepared.

Aged receivables analysis – 30 June 20X8

	Total £	Credit limit £	Current <30 days £	31–60 days £	61–90 days £	> 90 days £
Nerrington Engineering	4,484.04	5,000	2,138.77	994.60	1,350.67	–

Note that the 'current' portion is made up of Invoices 203903 and 203911, less the credit note 016452, which were all issued in June.

Activity 2: Preparation of an aged receivables analysis

You are working in the credit control department of Bourne Ltd. An extract from the company's aged receivables analysis at 30 September 20X4, together with information on the transactions that took place during October, is shown below.

Bourne Ltd

Aged Receivables Analysis – 30 September 20X4. Credit terms: 30 days.

Customer name and ref	Total amount	Current (<1 month)	O/s 1–2 months	O/s 2–3 months	O/s >3 months
Overton	£14,000	£5,000 B96		£9,000 B49	
Longparish	£7,000	£7,000 B95			
Stockbridge	£6,000			£3,000 B23	£3,000 B11
Andover	£15,000		£11,000 B72	£4,000 B42	
Greatley	£5,500				£5,500 B34
TOTAL	**£47,500**	**£12,000**	**£11,000**	**£16,000**	**£8,500**

Customer	Information for October 20X4
Overton	Paid invoice B49 £9,000. Invoice B96 remains unpaid. Invoice B101 £5,000 issued.
Longparish	Paid invoice B95 £7,000. Invoice B111 £6,600 issued.
Stockbridge	Paid invoice B11 £3,000. Invoice B23 remains unpaid. Invoice B102 £2,775 issued.
Andover	Paid invoice B42 £4,000. Invoice B72 £11,000 remains unpaid.
Greatley	Paid half invoice B34, balance remains unpaid.

Required

Prepare an aged receivables analysis as at 31 October 20X4.

Using the aged receivables analysis

The regular review of the aged receivables analysis should highlight the following potential problems:

- Credit limit exceeded
- Slow payers
- Recent debts cleared but older outstanding amounts
- Old amounts outstanding but no current trading

Credit limit exceeded

As we have already seen, when an order is placed by a credit customer the first step is to check whether the customer's credit limit will be exceeded as a result. However, this check may not always take place or, if the order is placed when the customer's account is not up to date, it may appear as if the credit limit will not be exceeded and therefore the sale is agreed.

If review of the aged receivables analysis indicates that a customer's credit limit has been exceeded then this must be investigated.

If a customer is highlighted in the aged receivables analysis as having exceeded their credit limit then, normally, the customer will be told that no further sales will be made to them until at least some of the outstanding balances have been paid. In some circumstances, liaison between the receivables ledger and the sales department may result in an increase in the customer's credit limit.

Activity 3: Recording invoices correctly

An invoice to a customer was not promptly recorded in the customer's receivables ledger account.

Required

Identify what effect there might be on the customer's account.

	✔
The balance may be too high	
The customer's credit limit may be exceeded	
Settlement discounts may be lost	
Further sales to the customer may be stopped	

Slow payers

Some businesses can be identified from the aged receivables listing as being slow payers: they always have amounts outstanding for, say, 31–60 days and 61–90 days, as well as current amounts.

In these cases consideration should be given to methods of encouraging the customer to pay earlier. This could be in the form of a reminder letter or telephone call or perhaps the offer of a settlement discount for earlier payment.

Recent debts cleared but older amount outstanding

If a customer is generally a regular payer and fairly recent debts have been cleared, but there is still an outstanding older amount, then this will normally indicate either a query over the amount outstanding or a problem with the recording of invoices, credit notes or payments received.

If there appears to be no communication from the customer about a queried invoice that would account for the old outstanding debt, then the invoice postings, credit note postings and payments received from that customer should be checked to ensure that there have been no errors which have resulted in the recording of this outstanding amount. If there appear to be no errors, then the customer should be contacted in order to find out what the problem is concerning payment of this particular amount.

Old amounts outstanding and no current trading

This situation would be of some concern for the credit control team. It would appear that the customer is no longer buying from the business but still owes money from previous purchases. In this case the customer should be contacted immediately and payment sought. If no contact can be made with the customer, or there is a genuine problem with payment (such as bankruptcy or liquidation) consideration should be given to writing off the debt as irrecoverable.

Illustration 3

Given below is an extract from the aged receivables analysis of the fuel division of SC Fuel and Glass at 30 June 20X8.

Aged receivables analysis – 30 June 20X8

	Total £	Credit limit £	Current <30 days £	31–60 days £	61–90 days £	> 90 days £
Pentagon Ltd	7,357.68	10,000	4,268.79	3,088.89		
White & Co	1,363.56	2,000	1,135.46		228.10	
Nantwich Ltd	3,745.24	5,000	732.34	1,983.36	1,029.54	
Bella Partners	4,836.47	4,000	2,295.36	2,541.11		
Manfred Paul	832.56	1,000				832.56

The position of each customer must be considered and any necessary action taken.

Pentagon Ltd — When the credit agreement with Pentagon Ltd is checked it is noted that this long-standing customer is allowed 60 days of credit from the invoice date, therefore there are no amounts overdue.

White & Co — The credit terms for this business are 30 days from the invoice date, therefore the amount over 60 days of £228.10 is certainly overdue. However, with no other overdue amounts, this might indicate that there is a query regarding this figure; the customer's correspondence file should be checked. If there appears to be no queried amount then there might have been an error in the posting to the account, which must also be checked.

Nantwich Ltd — The credit terms for this business are 30 days from the invoice date, therefore the vast majority of the debt is outstanding. This company appears to be a slow payer and consideration should be given to encouraging them to pay within the stated credit period.

Bella Partners — Credit terms of 30 days, therefore over half the debt is overdue. The customer has also exceeded their credit limit and the reason for this should be investigated. It may be decided to stop any further supplies to the customer until the overdue amounts are paid.

Manfred Paul — This is of great concern, as there has been no current trading but there is an old amount outstanding. The customer should be contacted immediately with a view to collection of the amount due.

The 80/20 rule

The 80/20 rule is that, in general, 80% of the value of amounts owed by customers will be represented by 20% of the customer accounts.

According to the 80/20 rule, if the largest accounts (making up 20% of customers) are reviewed frequently, this should mean that approximately 80% of the total of receivables balances are regularly reviewed.

The remaining smaller balances, making up only 20% of the receivables total, can then be reviewed on a less-frequent basis.

Materiality

Another approach when analysing receivables is to prioritise the receivables ledger by taking into account the materiality or significance of the debt. Thus overdue debts below a certain amount should be ignored until larger, more significant debts have been pursued as a priority.

This allows specific areas to be targeted by the credit control function of a business to minimise losses due to irrecoverable debts or to improve cash flow. It also takes into account that some debts may not be worth pursuing as the time and costs involved may outweigh the likely benefits.

Assessment focus point

When considering whether an item is material, always put this into context with additional information supplied. A customer failing to pay a £1,000 invoice may be material to a small business but, perhaps, not material to a large multinational corporation.

Measuring the average period of credit

It can be useful for a business to be able to determine the average period of credit taken by its customers in total. If these figures are compared over time then any improvement or deterioration of credit control procedures can be identified.

The most common method of measuring the average period of credit is using the accounts receivable collection period. This can be compared over time and also can be compared with the accounts payable payment period. If the accounts receivable collection period is consistently shorter than the accounts payable payment period, then this will aid liquidity.

Increase in credit limit

There will be occasions when a customer specifically requests an increase in credit limit. It may be that the customer wishes to place an order which will exceed the credit limit. The aged receivables listing can be a useful tool in making a decision about any increase in credit limit, as it allows the credit controller to see the trading history of the customer, whether or not they have kept within their current limit in the past and paid according to their credit terms.

Activity 4: Action to take

The aged receivables analysis for a business shows that a customer has £736.50 owing from the current period and £104.00 due from the 61/90-day period.

Required

Explain the course of action that should be taken concerning this customer.

3 Irrecoverable debts

The aged receivables analysis can also be used to identify debts which might be irrecoverable. These consist of **irrecoverable debts** and **doubtful debts**. Any debts that are not paid will, of course, have a negative impact on the cash flow of the organisation as working capital will be reduced by the comparative amount of balances unpaid.

An irrecoverable debt is one where it is almost certain that the monies will not be received. A doubtful debt is one where there is some doubt over the eventual receipt of the money, but it is not such a clear case as an irrecoverable debt. The reason for the distinction between the two is that in the financial accounting records an irrecoverable debt is written off, and no longer appears in the ledger or on the statement of financial position, whereas a doubtful debt has an allowance or a provision made against it – so it still appears in the ledger, and on the statement of financial position where it is netted-off against the receivables balance.

Identification of irrecoverable and doubtful debts

The following can be clues indicating a potential irrecoverable debt:

- Evidence of long-outstanding debts from the aged receivables analysis
- A one-off outstanding debt when more recent debts have been cleared
- Correspondence with customers
- Outstanding older debts and no current business with the customer
- A sudden or unexpected change in payment patterns
- Request for an extension of credit terms
- Press comment
- Information from the sales team

Illustration 4

Given again is the extract from the fuel division's aged receivables analysis at 30 June 20X8.

Aged receivables analysis – 30 June 20X8

	Total £	Credit limit £	Current <30 days £	31–60 days £	61–90 days £	> 90 days £
Pentagon Ltd	7,357.68	10,000	4,268.79	3,088.89		
White & Co	1,363.56	2,000	1,135.46		228.10	
Nantwich Ltd	3,745.24	5,000	732.34	1,983.36	1,029.54	
Bella Partners	4,836.47	4,000	2,295.36	2,541.11		
Manfred Paul	832.56	1,000				832.56

The two debts which may be under consideration are the old debts owing by White & Co and by Manfred Paul.

Upon investigation it is discovered that the amount of £228.10 is in dispute with White & Co as they have no record of having received this delivery of fuel. SC's despatch team are still trying to find evidence that the fuel was supplied but, as yet, they can find no delivery note to support the invoice that was sent out. This could be viewed as a doubtful debt as there is certainly some doubt as to whether this was, in fact, a valid sale or not.

Manfred Paul is an individual customer with whom SC has traded periodically. Upon contacting Manfred Paul it has been discovered that he has been declared bankrupt and has no funds to pay his suppliers. This debt will probably be declared an irrecoverable debt.

Information about potential irrecoverable debts

If a member of the credit control team discovers that a debt is highly likely to be classified as irrecoverable or doubtful then it will probably not be that person's responsibility to write the debt off or set up an allowance against it. This is normally the role of a more senior member of the accounting function, as this will impact on the preparation of the financial statements of a business.

Activity 5: Irrecoverable and doubtful debts

When a customer's account is overdue the amount involved may become an irrecoverable or a doubtful debt.

Required

Which of the following is correct about irrecoverable and doubtful debts?

	✓
An irrecoverable debt will not be received and an allowance is made	
A doubtful debt may be received but it is written off	
An irrecoverable debt may be received and an allowance is made	
A doubtful debt may not be received and an allowance is made	

Activity 6: Irrecoverable, doubtful debts and no action

At the year end 31 December 20X5 total receivables amount to £17,221.75.

This amount is owed between three customers and is analysed in the aged receivables analysis as below.

Aged receivables analysis – 31 December 20X5

	Total £	Credit limit £	Current <30 days £	31–60 days £	61–90 days £	> 90 days £
D. Layed Ltd	1,600.29	2,000			1,600.29	
Timely Plc	4,820.90	5,000	4,820.90			
Busted Ltd	10,800.56	10,000			2,644.15	8,156.41

Required

Identify in your opinion which accounts should be written off, have an allowance provided for or where no action is required.

	No action	Allowance for doubtful debt	Write-off as irrecoverable
D. Layed Ltd			
Timley Plc			
Busted Ltd			

Assessment focus point

Writing off a customer's account will impact on the financial statements but this should not prevent further chasing; if the debt is received at later date the amount can easily be written back into the books of account of the business.

VAT implications

When a debt is written off as irrecoverable the VAT element of the debt will be included with the amount outstanding from the customer. Cash flow issues arise as the business may have accounted for the VAT element to HM Revenue & Customs (HMRC).

VAT bad debt relief

When the business has accounted for the VAT to HMRC then bad debt relief can be used to claim back or net-off VAT suffered by the business.

VAT bad debt relief can be claimed when:

• The VAT has been accounted for to HMRC
• The debt has actually been written off as irrecoverable in the books of account
• The debt is over six months old

Illustration 5

A customer has gone bankrupt owing AB Ltd an invoice for £4,500 that includes VAT at 20%. The debt is over six months old and AB Ltd has previously passed on the VAT element of the invoice to HMRC. The total debt has been written off as irrecoverable in AB Ltd's books.

How much can be claimed under bad debt relief and how much should be written off as irrecoverable?

The VAT element of the invoice is £750 (4,500/1.2 × 0.20) and this can be claimed back from HMRC. The amount that should be written off as irrecoverable is £3,750 (4,500 – 750) as this is the net amount of the invoice. As £4,500 has already been written off in AB Ltd's books £750 needs to be written back so that the correct amount is accounted for.

Professional ethics and irrecoverable and doubtful debts

Writing off debts as irrecoverable will have an effect on reported profits and issues can arise when debts are written off in one period and then subsequently written back in another period in an attempt to smooth profits between accounting periods.

Accounting for debts should reflect the financial reality of the situation and be dealt with adhering to the fundamental ethical principles of integrity and objectivity. This means that accounting should be completed with honesty and without any conflict of interest when reporting results of a business.

4 Debt collection policy

Most businesses will have some sort of policy, whether formal or informal, regarding the collection of debts and the processes that will take place to chase up any outstanding amounts.

Debt collection process

The **debt collection process** starts with the sending out of the sales invoice on which the credit terms should be clearly stated. Thereafter, a variety of external communications would be sent to the customer to encourage them to pay within the credit terms and, for those overdue debts, a further series of reminders.

A typical debt collection process can be illustrated:

Invoice sent
|
Statement sent
|
Telephone reminder
|
Reminder letters
|
Stop list
|
External means of
debt collection

Sales invoice

Once a sale has been made a sales invoice can be sent to the customer. This should be promptly sent, as soon as the goods or services have been provided, and should clearly state the payment period agreed.

Statements

Most businesses will then send a monthly **statement** to the customer, showing the balance at the end of that month and how that is made up, including invoices, credit notes and payments received.

Telephone calls

An **overdue debt** is one which has not been paid within the stated credit period. Once a debt has become overdue it is common practice to telephone the customer to enquire about the situation, determine whether or not there is a query over the amount due and agree when the debt will be paid.

When making this type of telephone call, particular attention should be given to the following matters:

- Discussion with the customer should always be courteous.

- The precise amount of the debt should be pointed out, and the fact that it is overdue.

- It should be established whether there is any query with regard to the debt and, if so, any appropriate action agreed to resolve the query.

- If there is no query then a date for payment of the debt should be established.

It is important to keep precise notes of what has been agreed in a telephone conversation with a customer, as this may need to be confirmed by letter. For example, if a customer agrees over the telephone to clear an outstanding amount by paying in four instalments then this should be confirmed to the customer in writing.

Reminder letters

If there has been no response to telephone calls requesting payment of the overdue amount then this is followed up with a **reminder letter**.

This first reminder letter is designed to point out the facts – the amount outstanding – and as a reminder or encouragement to pay the amount due. As with all letters to customers it must be courteous and succinct as well as firm.

The reminder letter will be sent out when the debts are a certain amount of time overdue. The timescale of the reminder letter will depend upon the organisation's policy towards debt collection but usually it is sent out seven days after a debt becomes overdue. Accordingly, if an invoice is sent to a customer with 30-day credit terms, then the first reminder letter will be sent out 37 days after the invoice.

An example of a typical first reminder letter is given below:

Date

Dear Sir

Account No: 385635/A

I do not appear to have received payment of the invoices detailed below. I trust that this is an oversight and that you will arrange for immediate payment to be made. If you are withholding payment for any reason, please contact me urgently and I will be pleased to assist you.

Invoice No	Terms	Due date	Amount £

If you have already made payment please advise me and accept my apology for having troubled you.

Yours faithfully
Credit controller

Final reminder letters

If there is no response from the initial reminder letter then there will be little point in sending a second reminder letter. However, at this stage a telephone call might be useful to clear up any misunderstanding and to assess whether further action is required.

The options for the business at this point are generally:

- To put the debt into the hands of a debt collection agency

- To take the customer to court for payment

- To suspend any further sales to the customer by placing the customer on a **stop list** until payment is received

An example of a typical stop list letter is given below:

Date

Dear Sir

Account No: 385635/A

Further to our invoices detailed below, and our previous correspondence I do not appear to have received payment. I trust that this is an oversight and that you will arrange for immediate payment to be made. If you are withholding payment for any reason, please contact me urgently and I will be pleased to assist you.

Invoice No	Terms	Due date	Amount £

I regret that unless payment is received within the next seven days I will have no alternative but to stop any further sales on credit to you until the amount owing is cleared in full. If you have already made payment please advise me and accept my apology for having troubled you. Please note that if we are forced to take legal action you may become liable for the costs of such action which, if successful, may affect your future credit rating.

Yours faithfully

Management briefing notes

In addition to drafting letters to customers, the credit control function may also be requested to prepare **briefing notes** for senior management outlining any potential problems and the consequences (eg an irrecoverable debt) along with any actions taken. The key for briefing notes is to keep the communication short and to contain the relevant information surrounding any credit control issues identified.

Illustration 6

The glass division of SC Fuel and Glass has the following written policy for debt collection.

Debt collection policy

1   Invoices should be sent out on the same day as goods are delivered.

2   An aged analysis of receivables should be produced monthly.

3   Statements are sent to credit customers on the first working day of each month.

4   A reminder letter is sent when a debt is seven days overdue.

5   A telephone call to chase payment must be made when a debt is 14 days overdue.

6   When the debt is 30 days overdue, the customer will be placed on the stop list and a letter sent confirming this. A meeting should then be arranged with the customer in order to discuss the account position.

7   When the debt is 60 days overdue it will be placed in the hands of a debt collection agency or legal proceedings will be commenced, based upon the decision of the financial controller.

An invoice was sent to Yarrow Ltd, for £8,570 on 1 June on 30-day credit terms. This debt is still outstanding at 30 June.

The process that would follow, assuming that the money was not received, would be:

•   7 July – first reminder letter sent

•   14 July – telephone reminder

•   30 July – placed on stop list and final reminder letter sent. Meeting arranged to resolve the payment problem

•   29 August – decision taken regarding final treatment of overdue amount

Activity 7: Telephone calls to customers

One method of reminding customers to settle their accounts is the use of telephone calls.

Required

Explain the factors that are important when planning a telephone call to a customer regarding an overdue account.

Assessment focus point

Sometimes adhering to a credit or debt collection policy too closely can cause problems. For example, if a well-established customer is late in paying their account it would be good practice to check first with the chief credit controller before putting the account on stop. This can help to avoid any unnecessary bad feeling with the customer and potential loss of custom.

5 Example of a credit control policy and procedure

The following is an example of a typical credit control policy and procedure.

New accounts

1   One bank reference and two trade references are required.

2   A credit reference agency report and the last three years' published accounts for limited companies need to be analysed.

3   A credit reference agency report and the last three years' accounts for a sole trader need to be analysed.

Existing customers

4   A credit reference agency report to be obtained on an annual basis, together with the latest annual accounts from Companies House or directly from the customer.

5   A trading history review to be undertaken annually to review the performance against credit limits and terms of payment.

6   Annual review of usage of the customers' credit limit and to ensure that an outdated credit limit is not in existence.

Credit terms

7   Standard terms are 30 days from invoice. Any extension to be authorised by the finance director.

8   A 2% settlement discount to be offered to all accounts with a profit margin of 50% or greater.

Debt collection process

9   Invoices to be despatched on day of issue.

10   Statements to be despatched in the second week of the month.

11   Aged receivables analysis to be produced and reviewed on a weekly basis.

12   Reminder letter to be sent once an account is overdue.

13   Telephone chaser for accounts 15 days overdue.

14   Customer on stop list if no payment is received within five days of the telephone chaser.

15   Letter threatening legal action if payment not received within 30 days of the first letter.

16   Legal proceedings or debt collection agency instructed, subject to approval of the finance director.

17   Prepare a report suggesting an appropriate allowance for doubtful debts.

18   If, at any stage in the process, the customer is declared insolvent or bankrupt then contact the insolvency practitioner in order to register the debt and notify the financial accountant so that the VAT can be reclaimed.

Activity 8: Aged receivables action plan

The credit control policy of Kencorp Ltd and an extract from the company's aged receivables analysis are given below.

Credit control policy

1   Invoices must be issued on the same day as goods despatched.

2   An aged analysis of trade receivables is to be produced monthly.

3   Credit terms are strictly 30 days from the date of invoice.

4   Statements are despatched on the first working day of each month.

5   A reminder letter must be sent when debt is 14 days overdue.

6   A telephone call to chase payment must be made when a debt is 21 days overdue.

7   The customer is placed on the stop list when debt is 30 days overdue and a meeting arranged.

8   A letter threatening legal action will be sent when the debt is 45 days overdue.

9 Legal proceedings are to be commenced when a debt is 60 days overdue, subject to the agreement of the financial controller.

Aged receivables analysis – 30 June 20X6

	Total £	Credit limit £	Current <30 days £	31–60 days £	61–90 days £	> 90 days £
Castle Builders	10,800	12,000				10,800
DD DIY Ltd	6,800	10,000	5,200	1,200		400
AP Partners	3,250	4,000	1,000	1,000	1,250	
Gatfield Ltd	17,640	25,000	8,200	8,600	840	
Krane Ltd	21,200	20,000	8,900	12,300		
Crane Co	3,200	4,000	3,200			

Required

Suggest an action for each of Kencorp Ltd's customers and include any recommendations for an allowance for doubtful debts.

Chapter summary

- The benefit of offering credit to customers is the likely increase in sales. However, there are also costs of lost interest and potential irrecoverable debts. The role of the credit control function is to minimise these costs.

- The credit control function is involved in the ordering cycle in establishing customer credit status and offering credit terms and throughout the collection cycle.

- Every business will have its own credit control policies, terms and conditions regarding how and when payment is to be made by credit customers.

- When evaluating a customer's credit status the concerns are that the customer will pay within the stated credit terms and that the business will remain solvent.

- Credit assessment decisions need to be taken with the ethical principle of objectivity. This will mean that decisions will be reached without bias, conflict of interest or any undue influence.

- When either a potential new customer requests credit, or an existing customer requests an increase in credit limit, the credit controller will make use of internal and external information about the customer, in order to determine whether or not the request should be granted.

Keywords

- **Aged receivables analysis:** An analysis of each individual receivable's balance split into amounts that have been outstanding for particular periods of time.

- **Briefing notes:** Short notes that provide an outline for management on credit control issues and actions taken.

- **Credit limit:** The maximum amount that should be outstanding on a customer's receivable ledger account at any one point in time.

- **Debt collection process:** A process that outlines the steps an organisation will take to encourage payment from customers.

- **Doubtful debts:** Debts where there is some doubt over whether the monies due will eventually be received.

- **Irrecoverable debts:** Debts that will be written off.

- **Overdue debt:** A debt which has not been paid within the stated credit period

- **Reminder letter:** A letter sent to a customer encouraging payment of an overdue debt.

- **Statement:** Analysis of the amount due by a customer and the transactions on their account for the last period, which is periodically sent to the customer.

- **Stop list:** A list of customers to which goods should not be sold on credit.

Activity answers

Activity 1: Credit limits

	✓
Increasing goodwill with the customer	
Ensuring the cancellation of any settlement discount offered	
Loss of sale	
Increasing the risk of non-payment of the amount due	✓

The credit limit that is set for a credit customer will have been set by the credit controller as part of the assessment of the risk of the customer. Therefore if this credit limit is exceeded it is potentially increasing the risk that the business faces from these sales on credit.

Activity 2: Preparation of an aged receivables analysis

Bourne Ltd Aged receivables analysis as at 31 October 20X4

Customer name and ref	Total amount	Current < 1 month	O/s 1-2 months	O/s 2-3 months	O/s >3 months
Overton	£10,000	£5,000 B101	£5,000 B96		
Longparish	£6,600	£6,600 B111			
Stockbridge	£5,775	£2,775 B102			£3,000 B23
Andover	£11,000			£11,000 B72	
Greatley	£2,750				£2,750 B34
Total	**£36,125**	**£14,375**	**£5,000**	**£11,000**	**£5,750**

Activity 3: Recording invoices correctly

	✓
The balance may be too high	
The customer's credit limit may be exceeded	✓
Settlement discounts may be lost	
Further sales to the customer may be stopped	

If an invoice is not properly recorded in the customer's receivables ledger account then this may mean that the next time that the customer places an order the balance on the account is too low. When the credit limit is checked to ensure that it is not exceeded by the new order value, the sale might be authorised – even though the new order may in fact take the customer over the credit limit.

Activity 4: Action to take

As the customer has current amounts due, but no 30-to-61 day amounts due, it could be assumed that he was a regular payer; therefore the £104 due from 61-to-90 days was an amount that was being queried. The best course of action would be to check the customer's correspondence file to determine if this amount was being queried – and also to check that the amount was, in fact, due from this customer and that there were no errors in posting to the customer's account. Then a telephone call should be made to the customer to enquire why this overdue amount has not been paid.

Activity 5: Irrecoverable and doubtful debts

	✓
An irrecoverable debt will not be received and an allowance is made	
A doubtful debt may be received but it is written off	
An irrecoverable debt may be received and an allowance is made	
A doubtful debt may not be received and an allowance is made	✓

An irrecoverable debt is one where it is almost certain that the money is not going to be received, whereas a doubtful debt is one where there is some doubt over whether the money will be received – but no certainty. The importance of the distinction between an irrecoverable and a doubtful debt is in their respective accounting treatments. An irrecoverable debt is written off from the financial statements, whereas an allowance is made for a doubtful debt.

Activity 6: Irrecoverable, doubtful debts and no action

	No action	Allowance for doubtful debt	Write-off as irrecoverable
D. Layed Ltd		✓	
Timley Plc	✓		
Busted Ltd			✓

D. Layed Ltd is within its credit limit, however its outstanding balance is over 60 days old. This may indicate this company is having financial difficulties and this debt may be doubtful as to being settled.

Timley Plc's balance is within its credit limit and is current. No action required at this stage.

Busted Ltd has exceeded its credit limit and a substantial amount of the balance outstanding is now over 90 days. There is no current trading and it may be prudent to write off these amounts as irrecoverable.

Activity 7: Telephone calls to customers

When making a telephone call to discuss an overdue debt with a customer, the following factors are of particular importance:

- Discussion with the customer should always be courteous.

- The precise amount of the debt should be pointed out and the fact that it is overdue.

- It should be established whether there is any query with regard to the debt and, if so, any appropriate action should be agreed to resolve the query.

- If there is no query then a date for payment of the debt should be established.

- All of this should be recorded for future reference.

Activity 8: Aged receivables action plan

	Possible actions
Castle Builders	As the amount is over 60 days, refer to the financial controller to commence legal proceedings. The account should already be on stop and an allowance made for a doubtful debt.
DD DIY Ltd	As part of the account is over 21 days overdue a telephone call should be made to chase the account. The £400 may be a dispute and should be queried. An allowance for a doubtful debt can be made for the £400.
AP Partners	£2,250 is, in total, overdue. This account should be on stop as £1,250 is now over 30 days. A meeting needs to be arranged with the customer to discuss the operation of the account.
Gatfield Ltd	This customer has one of the largest credit limits and is within that limit. However, there are some amounts that are overdue and these need to be chased. Normally the account would be on stop but it may be prudent to try to obtain payment before putting it on stop, to retain the goodwill of the customer.
Krane Ltd	This customer has exceeded its credit limit and should be put on stop. A check should be carried out to ensure all transactions have been correctly recorded. The customer should be contacted to discuss the situation.
Crane Co	Customer is within its credit limit and its balance is current. No action is required at this stage.

Test your learning

1 If customer accounts in the receivables ledger are not kept accurately up to date then this can cause a number of problems.

   Which of the following is not one of those problems?

   A   Problem items may not be highlighted in the aged receivables listing.
   B   Incorrect statements may be sent out to customers.
   C   The correct goods may not be despatched to the customer.
   D   Orders may be taken which exceed the customer's credit limit.

2 A customer of a business has an outstanding balance on its receivables ledger account of £17,685 at 31 July. This balance is made up as follows:

		£
22 May	Inv 093106	2,184
3 June	Inv 093182	3,785
21 June	Inv 093265	4,839
2 July	Credit note 04623	(536)
5 July	Inv 093321	3,146
20 July	Inv 093346	4,267
		17,685

   The customer's name is Fording Ltd and the company has a credit limit of £20,000.

   Use the table below to complete the aged receivables analysis for this customer as at 31 July.

Customer	Total	Credit limit	Current <30 days	31-60 days	61-90 days	90 days
	£	£	£	£	£	£

3 **Which of the following might typically be highlighted by analysis of an aged receivables listing?**

   (i)   Slow payers
   (ii)   Settlement discounts taken
   (iii) Exceeding a credit limit
   (iv) Potential irrecoverable debts
   (v)   Credit terms
   (vi) Items in dispute

   A   (i), (ii), (iv) and (v)
   B   (iii), (iv), (v) and (vi)
   C   (i), (iii), (iv) and (v)
   D   (i), (iii), (iv) and (vi)

4   Given below are extracts from an aged receivables analysis for a company at 30 September:

	Total £	Credit limit £	Current <30 days £	31–60 days £	61–90 days £	>90 days £
Kerry & Co	5,389	8,000	4,999		390	
Marshall Ltd	16,378	15,000	16,378			
Leyton Ltd	5,377	10,000	1,854	1,757	1,766	

Credit terms are that payment is due within 30 days of the invoice date.

For each customer, state what the aged receivables listing might indicate about that customer and what, if any, action might be required.

Customer	Comment and action
Kerry & Co	
Marshall Ltd	
Leyton Ltd	

5   **What information available to the credit control team might indicate the existence of an irrecoverable or doubtful debt?**

6   A company has a policy of granting credit terms of 30 days from the invoice date. Once an invoice is seven days overdue, a telephone call is made to the customer to enquire about the debt. Once an invoice is 14 days overdue, a reminder letter is sent to the customer. Once an invoice is 30 days overdue, the customer is placed on the stop list and a letter is sent informing them of this.

Given below is an extract from the company's aged receivables listing at 30 June.

	Total £	Credit limit £	Current <30 days £	31–60 days £	61–90 days £	>90 days £
Travis Ltd	4,678	5,000		4,678		
Muse Ltd	3,557	5,000	2,669	888		
Keane Ltd	6,248	8,000	5,145		1,103	

- The balance owing by Travis Ltd is made up of invoice number 467824 dated 15 May.

- Invoice number 467899 to Muse Ltd for £2,669 was dated 2 June and invoice number 467831 for £888 was dated 23 May.

- Invoice number 467781 to Keane Ltd for £1,103 was dated 22 April.

For each customer determine what action, if any, is necessary according to the credit collection policy and draft any letters that might be necessary to send to these customers.

Test your learning: answers

Chapter 1 – Managing the granting of credit

1   D   (ii) and (iv)

2   D   Customer places order. (This is a main element of the ordering cycle.)

3   Net 14 days, 3% discount for payment within 7 days.

4   C   (i), (iv), (v)

5   Credit circles are an external source of information, making use of knowledge from other companies which may have customers in common.

Chapter 2 – Granting credit to customers

1   C   Credit should be granted if further information is positive.

2   The information provided in the trade reference looks fairly positive in that SK Traders offers monthly payment terms which are only occasionally overrun. However, the amount of credit offered is only £8,000, whereas Caterham Ltd has applied to you for credit of £15,000.

   In conjunction with, perhaps, another trade reference and other internal and external information about Caterham Ltd, this trade reference may give you some confidence in the company.

3   Credit reference agencies can provide a variety of information about companies and individuals, which may include the following:

   - Historical financial statements
   - Directors' details
   - Payment history
   - Details of any insolvency proceedings or bankruptcy orders
   - Bankers' opinions
   - Credit rating

4   C   Annual financial statements

5

	20X9	20X8
Gross profit margin (%)	22.00	21.28
Operating profit margin (%)	12.00	11.70
Current ratio	0.54	0.66
Quick ratio	0.30	0.42
Accounts payable payment period (days)	74.87	79.41
Interest cover (times)	4.00	5.50

6

ACORN ENTERPRISES

Finance Partner

Little Partners

Date

Dear Sir

Re: Request for credit facilities

Thank you for your enquiry regarding the provision of credit facilities to yourselves for £8,000 of credit on 60-day terms. We have taken up your bank and trade references and examined your latest set of financial statements.

Although your references are satisfactory we have some concerns about your profitability and liquidity. Clearly, your overall profitability and liquidity position have improved since 20X7 but their levels are still lower than we would normally expect in order to grant a credit facility.

However, due to your bank and trade references, we are happy to offer you a credit facility for six months, at the end of which time the movement on your account will be reviewed and the position re-assessed. The credit limit that we can offer you initially would be £3,000 and the payment terms are strictly 30 days from the invoice date.

Thank you for your interest in our company and we look forward to trading with you on the basis set out above.

Yours faithfully

Jo Wilkie

Credit manager

7

Finance Director

Dawn Ltd

Date

Dear Sir

Re: Request for credit facilities

Thank you for your enquiry regarding the provision of credit facilities to yourselves for £5,000 of credit on 30-day terms. We have taken up your trade references and examined your latest set of financial statements.

Unfortunately we are concerned about your levels of profitability, gearing and liquidity in the most recent year, and also have some concerns about one of the trade references from Johannesson Partners.

On balance, we are not in a position to grant your request for trade credit at the current time, although we would, of course, be delighted to trade with you on a cash basis. If you do not wish to trade on this basis and would like to enquire about credit terms in the future, then we would be delighted to examine your current year's financial statements when they are available.

Thank you for your interest shown in our business.

Yours faithfully

Credit controller

Chapter 3 - Legislation and credit control

1   D   Agreement, value and intention to create legal relations

2   Alan cannot insist on purchasing the car for £3,000 as the advertisement is an invitation to treat, not an offer. When Alan answers the advertisement he is making an offer to purchase the car for £3,000 – which can be accepted or rejected by the seller.

3   The business does not have to supply the goods at £15,000, as the additional term for delivery the next day is a counter-offer which rejects the original offer.

4   A   A fundamental term of a contract

5   B   Payment for part of the contract performed

6   C   Payment by a third party

7   A 'retention of title' clause is a clause included in contracts stating that the buyer does not obtain ownership until payment is made.

8   The eight principles of good practice of the Data Protection Act are that personal information must be:

- Fairly and lawfully processed

- Processed for limited purposes

- Adequate, relevant and not excessive

- Accurate and up-to-date

- Not kept for longer than necessary

- Processed in line with the data subject's rights

- Kept securely

- Not transferred to countries outside the EU unless such data is adequately protected in those countries.

9   The seven rights for data subjects under the Data Protection Act are:

- The right to subject access

- The right to prevent processing

- The right to prevent processing for direct marketing

- Rights in relation to automated decision taking

- The right to compensation

- The right to rectification, blocking, erasure and destruction

- The right to ask the Commissioner to assess whether the Act has been contravened

Chapter 4 – Methods of credit control

1   C   21.3%

Cost of discount $= \dfrac{2}{100-2} \times \dfrac{365}{45-10} \times 100$

$= \quad 21.3\%$

2   C   Without recourse factoring does cover irrecoverable debts

3   A   Advance of cash (this is a benefit not a cost)

4   Any two of the following:

- A whole turnover policy, where either the whole receivables ledger is covered but the amount paid out for any irrecoverable debt is only, say, 80% of the claim; or 80% of the receivables ledger is covered for their entire amount and any claim on these would be paid in full.

- An annual aggregate excess policy, where irrecoverable debts are insured in total above an agreed limit or excess.

- A specific receivables policy, where only specific receivables ledger customers are insured for the irrecoverable debt risk.

5. £1,800 will be claimed under credit insurance and £200 written off as irrecoverable.

    (£2,400/1.2 × 0.20) = £400 VAT. The net value of the invoice is £2,000 (£2,400 – £400). 90% × £2,000 = £1,800 to be claimed under credit insurance and £200 to be written off as irrecoverable.

Chapter 5 – Managing the supply of credit

1   C   The correct goods may not be despatched to the customer

        This is not a problem caused by inaccurate customer accounts in the receivables ledger, because the goods will be despatched before the receivables ledger is written up – so despatch will not be affected.

2

Customer	Total £	Credit limit £	Current <30 days £	31-60 days £	61-90 days £	90 days £
Fording Ltd	17,685	20,000	6,877	8,624	2,184	

3   D   (i), (iii), (iv) and (vi)

4

Customer	Comment and action
Kerry & Co	The vast majority of this customer's debt is current, with a relatively small amount outstanding in 61-to-90 days. This may indicate that there was some dispute or error about this outstanding amount, which should be investigated.
Marshall Ltd	This customer has exceeded its credit limit, which should be investigated. However the balance is all current and, if this is a valued and reliable customer, it may be considered necessary to increase the credit limit to facilitate higher levels of trading.
Leyton Ltd	This customer would appear to be a persistently late payer with approximately one-third of its total debt spread over each month for the last three months. The credit controller will need to re-affirm the credit terms of 30 days with the customer and, possibly, offer some incentive for earlier payment such as a settlement discount.

5   Information that might be available to the credit control team which might indicate an irrecoverable or doubtful debt includes:

    • Evidence of long-outstanding debts from the aged receivables analysis
    • A one-off outstanding debt, when more recent debts have been cleared
    • Correspondence with receivables
    • Outstanding older debts and no current business with the customer

- A sudden or unexpected change in payment patterns
- Request for an extension of credit terms
- Press comment
- Information from the sales team

6 **Travis Ltd**

This amount is 14 days overdue and therefore a reminder letter must be sent to the customer.

Purchase ledger manager

Travis Ltd

30 June

Dear Sir

I do not appear to have received payment of the invoice detailed below. I trust that this is an oversight and that you will arrange for immediate payment to be made. If you are withholding payment for any reason, please contact me urgently and I will be pleased to assist you.

Invoice No	Terms	Due date	Amount £
467824	30 days	14 June	4,678.00

If you have already made payment please advise me and accept my apology for having troubled you.

Yours faithfully

Credit Controller

Muse Ltd

The invoice number 467831, for £888, is 7 days overdue and therefore a telephone call is necessary to the purchase ledger manager explaining that the amount is overdue, determining whether there is any query with the amount and agreeing a date for payment of the overdue amount.

Keane Ltd

The invoice for £1,103 is over 2 months overdue and should be investigated. Furthermore the policy is that once an amount is 30 days overdue the customer is put on the stop list. It would appear that this has not happened, as Keane Ltd has recent amounts (<30 days) due totalling £5,145.

A letter would be sent to the financial controller of Keane Ltd.

Financial Controller

Keane Ltd

Date

Dear Sir

Further to our invoice detailed below, I do not appear to have received payment. I trust that this is an oversight and that you will arrange for immediate payment to be made. If you are withholding payment for any reason, please contact me urgently and I will be pleased to assist you.

Invoice No	Terms	Due date	Amount £
467781	30 days	22 May	1,103.00

I regret that, unless payment is received within the next seven days, I will have no alternative but to stop any further sales on credit to you until the amount owing is cleared in full. If you have already made payment please advise me and accept my apology for having troubled you.

Yours faithfully

Credit Controller

Glossary of terms

It is useful to be familiar with interchangeable terminology including IFRS and UK GAAP (generally accepted accounting principles).

Below is a short list of the most important terms you are likely to use or come across, together with their international and UK equivalents.

UK term	International term
Profit and loss account	**Statement of profit or loss (or statement of profit or loss and other comprehensive income)**
Turnover or Sales	Revenue or Sales Revenue
Operating profit	Profit from operations
Reducing balance depreciation	Diminishing balance depreciation
Depreciation / depreciation expense(s)	Depreciation charge(s)
Balance sheet	**Statement of financial position**
Fixed assets	Non-current assets
Net book value	Carrying amount
Tangible assets	Property, plant and equipment
Stocks	Inventories
Trade debtors or Debtors	Trade receivables
Prepayments	Other receivables
Debtors and prepayments	Trade and other receivables
Cash at bank and in hand	Cash and cash equivalents
Long-term liabilities	Non-current liabilities
Trade creditors or creditors	Trade payables
Accruals	Other payables
Creditors and accruals	Trade and other payables
Capital and reserves	Equity (limited companies)
Profit and loss balance	Retained earnings
Cash flow statement	**Statement of cash flows**

Accountants often have a tendency to use several phrases to describe the same thing! Some of these are listed below:

Different terms for the same thing
Nominal ledger, main ledger or general ledger
Subsidiary ledgers, memorandum ledgers
Subsidiary (sales) ledger, sales ledger
Subsidiary (purchases) ledger, purchases ledger

Bibliography

Association of Accounting Technicians (2014) *AAT Code of Professional Ethics.* London, AAT.

Consumer Credit Act 2006. (2006) SI 2006/14. London, The Stationery Office.

Consumer Rights Act 2015. (2015) SI 2015/94. London, The Stationery Office.

Data Protection Act 1998. (1998) SI 1998/29. London, The Stationery Office.

Late Payment of Commercial Debts (Interest) Act 1998. (1998) SI 1998/20. London, The Stationery Office.

Trade Descriptions Act 1968. (1968) SI 1968/29. London, The Stationery Office.

Notes

Notes

Notes

REVIEW FORM

How have you used this Course Book?
(Tick one box only)

☐ Self study

☐ On a course_____

☐ Other _____

Why did you decide to purchase this Course Book? *(Tick one box only)*

☐ Have used BPP materials in the past

☐ Recommendation by friend/colleague

☐ Recommendation by a college lecturer

☐ Saw advertising

☐ Other _____

During the past six months do you recall seeing/receiving either of the following?
(Tick as many boxes as are relevant)

☐ Our advertisement in Accounting Technician

☐ Our Publishing Catalogue

Which (if any) aspects of our advertising do you think are useful?
(Tick as many boxes as are relevant)

☐ Prices and publication dates of new editions

☐ Information on Course Book content

☐ Details of our free online offering

☐ None of the above

Your ratings, comments and suggestions would be appreciated on the following areas of this Course Book.

	Very useful	Useful	Not useful
Chapter overviews	☐	☐	☐
Introductory section	☐	☐	☐
Quality of explanations	☐	☐	☐
Illustrations	☐	☐	☐
Chapter activities	☐	☐	☐
Test your learning	☐	☐	☐
Keywords	☐	☐	☐

	Excellent	Good	Adequate	Poor
Overall opinion of this Course Book	☐	☐	☐	☐

Do you intend to continue using BPP Products?   ☐ Yes ☐ No

Please note any further comments and suggestions/errors on the reverse of this page and return it to: Nisar Ahmed, AAT Head of Programme, BPP Learning Media Ltd, FREEPOST, London, W12 8AA.

Alternatively, the Head of Programme of this edition can be emailed at: nisarahmed@bpp.com

REVIEW FORM (continued)

TELL US WHAT YOU THINK

Please note any further comments and suggestions/errors below